Crime Fiction

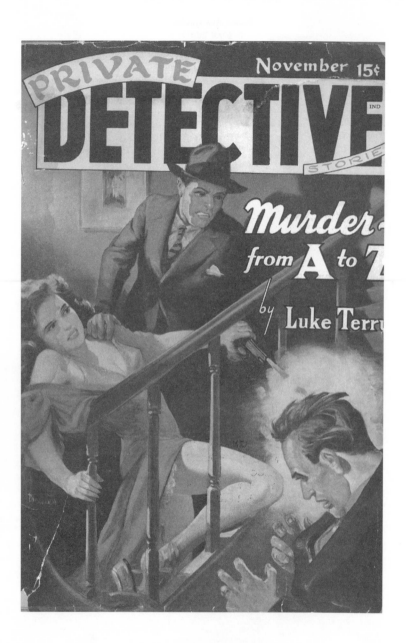

PRIVATE DETECTIVE

*from the cover of the issue of November 1941
by courtesy of Peter Haining*

Crime Fiction
from Poe to the Present

Martin Priestman

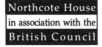
Northcote House
in association with the
British Council

Cover picture: Sherlock Holmes, from an illustration by Sidney Paget for 'The Adventure of the Abbey Grange' from *Strand* magazine, September 1904 reproduced, with the frontispiece, from *Mystery! An Illustrated History of Crime and Detective Fiction* by Peter Haining (Souvenir Press, 1977), by kind permission of the author.

© Copyright 1998 by Martin Priestman

First published in 1998 by Northcote House Publishers Ltd, Plymbridge House, Estover Road, Plymouth PL6 7PY, United Kingdom.
Tel: +44 (01752) 202368 Fax: +44 (01752) 202330.

British Library Cataloguing-in-Publication Data
A catalogue record for this book is available from the British Library

ISBN 0-7463-0854-X

Typeset by PDQ Typesetting, Newcastle-under-Lyme
Printed and bound in the United Kingdom

Contents

Acknowledgements

I would like to thank the students on the Detective Fiction course at Roehampton Institute London down the years; also Helen Kay, Simon Edwards, Louise Sylvester, Kevin McCarron, Sarah Turvey, Michael Newton and, for much crucial advice and support, Nicola Humble. I would also like to thank Brian Hulme and Joanna Jellinek of Northcote House for their unfailing kindness and helpfulness.

A Chronology

Since the defining dates of a genre are largely subjective, I list below what seem to me some of the main examples of the types of work discussed in this study. Someone else would undoubtedly have compiled a different list.

1794	William Godwin, *Caleb Williams*.
1829	François Eugène Vidocq, *Mémoires*.
	Sir Robert Peel founds Metropolitan Police.
1830	Edward Bulwer-Lytton, *Paul Clifford*.
1832	Bulwer-Lytton, *Eugene Aram*.
1834	Harrison Ainsworth, *Rookwood*.
1838	Charles Dickens, *Oliver Twist*.
1839	Ainsworth, *Jack Sheppard: A Romance of the Robber-Hero*.
1841	Edgar Allan Poe, 'The Murders in the Rue Morgue'.
1842	Detective Police set up in Britain.
1845	Poe, 'The Purloined Letter'.
1850–3	Dickens praises Detective Police in *Household Words* articles.
1860	Wilkie Collins, *The Woman in White*.
1862	Mary Elizabeth Braddon, *Lady Audley's Secret*.
1866	Emile Gaboriau, *L'Affaire Lerouge*.
1868	Collins, *The Moonstone*.
1869	Gaboriau, *Monsieur Lecoq*.
1878	Anna K. Green, *The Leavenworth Case*.
1886	Fergus Hume, *The Mystery of a Hansom Cab*.
1887	Arthur Conan Doyle, *A Study in Scarlet*.
1890	Doyle, *The Sign of Four*.
1892	Doyle, *The Adventures of Sherlock Holmes*.
	Israel Zangwill, *The Big Bow Mystery*.

1897	Arthur Morrison, *The Dorrington Deed-Box*.
1901	Rudyard Kipling, *Kim*.
1902	Doyle, *The Hound of the Baskervilles*.
1903	Erskine Childers, *The Riddle of the Sands*.
1907	Gaston Leroux, *Le Mystère de la chambre jaune*.
1911	G. K. Chesterton, *The Innocence of Father Brown*.
1912	R. Austin Freeman, *The Singing Bone*.
1913	E. C. Bentley, *Trent's Last Case*.
1915	John Buchan, *The Thirty-Nine Steps*.
1920	Agatha Christie, *The Mysterious Affair at Styles*.
	'Sapper', *Bulldog Drummond*.
1926	Christie, *The Murder of Roger Ackroyd*.
	Joseph T. Shaw edits *Black Mask* magazine.
1927	Doyle, *The Case-Book of Sherlock Holmes* (last of the series).
	Dorothy L. Sayers, *Unnatural Death*.
1929	Anthony Berkeley, *The Poisoned Chocolates Case*.
	W. R. Burnett, *Little Caesar*.
	Dashiell Hammett, *Red Harvest*.
1930	Christie, *The Murder at the Vicarage* (first Miss Marple novel).
1931	Francis Iles, *Malice Aforethought*.
1934	Hammett, *The Thin Man*.
	Rex Stout, *Fer de lance*.
1935	Sayers, *Gaudy Night*.
	John Dickson Carr, *The Hollow Man*.
	Ngaio Marsh, *Enter a Murderer*.
	Nicholas Blake, *A Question of Proof*.
1936	James M. Cain, *Double Indemnity*.
1937	Margery Allingham, *Dancers in Mourning*.
1938	Michael Innes, *Lament for a Maker*.
1939	Raymond Chandler, *The Big Sleep*.
	James Hadley Chase, *No Orchids for Miss Blandish*.
	Geoffrey Household, *Rogue Male*.
1942	Jorge Luis Borges, *Six Problems for Don Isidro Parodi*.
1943	Graham Greene, *The Ministry of Fear*.
1947	Ross Macdonald, *Blue City*.
1949	Patricia Highsmith, *Strangers on a Train*.
1950	Christie, *A Murder is Announced*.
1951	Josephine Tey, *The Daughter of Time*.

1952	Allingham, *The Tiger in the Smoke.*
1953	Chandler, *The Long Goodbye.*
	Ian Fleming, *Casino Royale.*
	Alain Robbe-Grillet, *Les Gommes.*
1962	P. D. James, *Cover her Face.*
1963	John le Carré, *The Spy Who Came in from the Cold.*
1964	Ruth Rendell, *From Doon with Death.*
1971	Frederick Forsyth, *The Day of the Jackal.*
	Macdonald, *The Underground Man.*
1972	James, *An Unsuitable Job for a Woman.*
1977	Rendell, *A Judgement in Stone.*
1980	Elmore Leonard, *City Primeval.*
1982	Sara Paretsky, *Indemnity Only.*
1984	Barbara Wilson, *Murder in the Collective.*
1985	Gillian Slovo, *Death by Analysis.*
1986	Sue Grafton, *A is for Alibi.*
1988	Paul Auster, *The New York Trilogy.*
1989	Elizabeth George, *Payment in Blood.*
	Robert Harris, *The Silence of the Lambs.*
1990	Patricia Cornwell, *Postmortem.*
1992	Walter Mosley, *White Butterfly.*
	Peter Høeg, *Smilla's Sense of Snow* (trans. 1993).
1995	James Ellroy, *American Tabloid.*
	Minette Walters, *The Dark Room.*

Introduction

A large part of the world's fiction concerns crime of some kind, so this brief study would have its work cut out if it aimed to be comprehensive. Fortunately, as a self-conscious genre, the detection-based 'whodunnit' firmly separated itself off once and for all from the rest of literature in 1841 with Edgar Allan Poe's 'The Murders in the Rue Morgue'. From then to now, the basic formula of this single short story has been endlessly reworked in a literary genre of astonishing stability, coherence and continuing popularity.

Poe's tradition has, however, run alongside and often intertwined with other ways of writing about crime, which are less easily pinned down to a single point of origin. In these forms, while detection might be one source of interest, it either accompanies or is replaced by others designed to involve us in a present action rather than just the resolving of a past mystery. In an essay to be discussed further in Chapter 1, Tsvetan Todorov firmly contrasts such 'thrillers' with the detective whodunnit in ways which I shall loosely follow in the categories adopted in this book.

Within this categorization, the whodunnit is primarily concerned with unravelling past events which either involve a crime or seem to do so. The present action is largely static, and major attention is given to the detecting activity itself, which may be performed by virtually anyone – police or amateur – who enjoys the final approval of the law.

In the thriller, the action is primarily in the present tense of the narrative. In one branch, which I call the *noir* thriller, we identify with characters who consciously exceed the law, whether in their whole lifestyles or through specific actions. In another, which I call the anti-conspiracy thriller, the protagonists confront a powerful conspiracy of wrongdoers without the guaranteed support of the forces of law and order. This group includes most spy fiction as well as much adventure fiction in which heroes match their powers against villains.

Between the detective whodunnit and the thriller, there is a hybrid form which can be most clearly described as the 'detective thriller'. This divides our interest between solving a past mystery and following a present action in which the protagonists may confront a dangerous conspiracy alone, or step outside the law, or both. This type includes most private-eye fiction, where the detective often has problematic relations with a 'law' which is sometimes itself in cahoots with a 'conspiracy'.

Because the whodunnit includes such a bulk of material, I have divided my discussion into two chapters on a simple chronological basis, before and after the First World War. Chapters 3 and 4 discuss the *noir* and anti-conspiracy thriller, and Chapter 5 the detective thriller. There is no implication of an overall chronological 'progression' between these four forms: while the last arguably starts later than the others, all four have long existed and flourished concurrently. Sometimes they overlap both with each other and with other types of fiction: examples of this, and their possible significance, are discussed in the Conclusion.

For the rest of this introduction, it will be useful to look a little further into some of the implications of the terms often applied to the various branches of crime fiction, and my reasons for adopting those I have.

The range of possible terms currently in use for what I have called the detective whodunnit betrays some uncertainty as to what aspects deserve most emphasis. Poe's name – 'tale of ratiocination' – never caught on, but the current American term, 'mystery', accurately identifies the puzzle element of the form – a puzzle addressed to the reader as well as the protagonists – though it leaves the question of a criminal element moot and allows a certain merging with gothic and supernatural modes through other meanings of 'mystery'. The more tongue-in-cheek term 'whodunnit' focuses attention on the crucial drive to identify the perpetrator of a specific crime, though it also introduces a strangely skewed class-element, suggesting that such questions are only for the uneducated. This sits oddly with the form's rather staid, genteel image, as sometimes conveyed in such alternative phrases as 'classic' and 'Golden Age'.

The more neutral term 'detective fiction' avoids these problems, but contains a significant ambiguity depending on whether 'detective' is read as a noun or an adjective: is it fiction which detects, or fiction with detectives in it? If the former, we return to the useful formal emphasis of 'mystery', allotting a key role for the reader; if the latter, we may either be tempted to include thrillers and other texts where detectives are present but not pivotal, or feel implicitly invited to fix our ideas on the character and role of the detective as a personality. For some traditionalists, this character-based emphasis can lead to the claim that only a certain type of detective – private or amateur, or possessing certain mannerisms – fits the bill. More usefully, however, the emphasis on the detective protagonist can serve to remind us that the genre could not have come into being before the early-nineteenth-century emergence of a social formation which saw the need for such a role and hence created actual detectives, who were of course primarily members of the police.

It seems to me that most of these implications have some place in the consideration of the genre, and accordingly I have adopted the belt-and-braces approach of combining the two most familiar to British readers, preserving the suggestive class-confusions of 'whodunnit' and only reluctantly dropping the formally precise 'mystery' because it remains a chiefly American usage.

Of the other terms I have adopted, the thriller is clearly so named because its chief aim, or at least effect, is suspense: a painful but 'thrilling' state of anticipation rather than mere curiosity about past events. *Noir*, the term I have used to describe the criminal-centred thriller, is taken from the French term *film noir*, describing films featuring such plots and also identifying a certain 'dark' quality in formal presentation as well as content. Somehow, even in English-language discussions of culture, the term has become so prevalent and influential that it seems inevitable to describe the ambiguous *frisson* of watching assorted transgressors 'just like us' on the downhill slide.

The more plodding term 'anti-conspiracy thriller' is my own coinage as far as I know, but is at least briefer than 'suspense story with protagonists we approve of', which is more or less all

3

it is intended to mean. Though it may seem to detract attention from the single, towering antagonist who sometimes comes to dominate such works, the word 'conspiracy' is there to denote the scale of the opposition to be confronted by a protagonist whose outnumbering (even if only by one, but often by an array of henchpeople) is usually a given of the form.

The term 'detective thriller' aims chiefly to indicate the joint parentage of a form also often known as 'private-eye fiction' or adjectivally just as the 'hardboiled'. The second of these terms, however, is often just as appropriate to the *noir* thriller, while the first evokes a rather too precise image of the protagonist's professional status as a private detective for hire, something which is usually the case in this form but does not absolutely define it. Todorov's term 'suspense novel' seems simply an alternative name for 'thriller': my term tries to complete the marriage of true genres towards which his brief essay usefully points. Once brought into being, however, the form has not needed to look back over its shoulder at its origins: it is a major crystallization of several of the richer possibilities of crime fiction in its own right.

Finally, a brief word about the limits I have set myself in this book. Though all the types of crime fiction discussed have been practised internationally, for reasons of space I have confined myself to discussing British and American writing except where a foreign-language writer makes a really decisive impact on the Anglo-American tradition. With such a potentially infinite range of texts to cover even within this restriction, I have repeatedly had to make discussion of a single one stand in for consideration of a whole range of others, even in the case of some clearly very significant authors. And, while even briefer references to many authors can hope only to gesture at their possible place in my argument, there are of course many more whom there has simply been no space to name at all.

1

The Detective Whodunnit from Poe to World War I

The detective whodunnit focuses primarily on identifying the perpetrator of a crime which for most of the story or novel already lies in the past. As Tsvetan Todorov has pointed out in his useful essay 'The Typology of Detective Fiction', this placing of the major event in a concealed 'first story' which has taken place prior to most of the narrated action compels the 'second story' of the latter to be relatively static, focusing our attention on a slow process of uncovering (and sometimes on the practical difficulties of narrative itself), rather than on any very meaningful or character-revealing action. The only such 'action' to which we can look forward – the final unmasking of the perpetrator – can happen only once, at the very end, which is also the moment when the hitherto concealed 'first story' comes to be told in its entirety. As Todorov also argues, however, this strangely split-level narrative approach is only an intensification of the split in all fiction between what Russian Formalist critics, following Aristotle, have defined as 'story' (what is actually supposed to have happened) and 'plot' (the way we are told about it).[1]

Since the whodunnit makes a particular use of what may be seen as the raw material of narrative in general, it is not surprising that many apparent antecedents for it can be found before its generally recognized inception, in 1841, with Poe's 'The Murders in the Rue Morgue'. One of the most striking such antecedents is Sophocles's tragedy *Oedipus the King*, in which the hero, Oedipus, conducts a series of interrogations in his official kingly role to unmask the murderer of his predecessor King Laius. Through a meticulously plotted trail of evidence, it finally becomes clear that he himself was the unwitting killer in circumstances famously also involving parricide and incest. With the revelation comes punishment – self-punishment in this case, but it is arguable that purely as a detective Oedipus has done all the most rigorous whodunnit reader could demand, and, through the apparently alien device of the baffled chorus, Sophocles even ensures a proto-Watson-like channelling of maximum audience attention to the single issue of 'who done it?'

Perhaps the only element crucially separating *Oedipus* from detective fiction proper is that of repeatability. Put simply, the audience knew from legend that Oedipus was the culprit, but were still absorbed and moved by the process by which this was being revealed to them. With later tragedies such as Shakespeare's *Hamlet*, the first audiences might indeed have spent part of the time in suspense over Claudius's precise degree of guilt, which the hero spends considerable energy in proving; nonetheless, the play's great fame and status since have ensured that the bare knowledge of the 'story' has little effect on current audiences' absorption in the 'plot' of the process by which it is finally brought fully to light. Clearly, in both tragedies, the plotting of an intensely moving process of uncovering is itself an 'action' of sufficient interest to survive pre-knowledge of the 'story' being uncovered.

With detective fiction, this is arguably not the case. W. H. Auden, a great fan, stated that the impossibility of rereading detective stories was such that 'If, as sometimes happens, I start reading one and find after a few pages that I have read it before, I cannot go on'.[2] This apparently essential disposability has perhaps helped to ensure that a form which is often meticulously clever on many narrative and stylistic levels encounters a kind of glass ceiling when it attempts to claim serious literary status: how can a text be held up as a shining example of plot, or indeed of anything related to the final outcome (such as character or stylistic ambiguity), when it is a kind of cardinal sin against the form to reveal to others – or even to recall for oneself – what that plot or that outcome actually is?

Despite an honoured tradition of 'not giving away the end' when writing about whodunnits, a serious study of the genre really has no choice: the texts cannot be discussed at all from a structural point of view apart from the endings which give them their shape and point. This is particularly the case with works

6

whose element of surprise is so striking as to constitute a kind of species-mutation in the evolution of the form. It is thus with only token reluctance that I now proceed to give away the plot of the short story which started it all, Poe's 'The Murders in the Rue Morgue'.

After a lengthy disquisition on the difference between mere ingenuity and true analysis, we are introduced to C. Auguste Dupin, a scion of decaying aristocracy whom the anonymous narrator met in a bookshop and with whom he now shares a Paris flat. As an instance of Dupin's analytic skill, a night-walk is described in which he accurately deduces the narrator's train of thought, from small body-language indications alone. We then shift to the narrative proper, beginning with the pair reading a lengthy newspaper report of the apparent murder of two women in an upstairs apartment: the neighbours all heard 'two voices' arguing with each other before the door was broken in and the corpses discovered, in a room to which there was apparently no other possible entry. Because of a vaguely stated acquaintance with the only suspect (a bank clerk who had visited the women earlier), Dupin decides to take an interest in the case, and visits the premises. He then stops off to place an advertisement in a daily newspaper, and once back home tells the narrator to stand by with pistols at the ready. At the predicted time a sailor arrives and, confronted by the pistols, brokenly confesses that an orang-utan he was trying to tame broke loose, swung into the Rue Morgue room via a window-shutter, killed the women and escaped, allowing the window to lock itself behind him thanks to a concealed catch. While unable to swing into the room himself, the sailor witnessed the whole scene from a lightning-rod, and it was his and the ape's voice in furious altercation the witnesses heard. At the end of the story, the sailor and the suspected clerk are both exonerated and the ape recaptured and exhibited in a zoo.

While this more or less accounts for the external action, most of the excitement of the story consists in Dupin's explanations of his various deductions, from the initial mind-reading to his reasons for concluding that the women must have been killed by an orang-utan, which must have escaped from a sailor who would be bound to peruse the newspaper 'found' column in which Dupin had inserted an advertisement claiming to have found the ape. By eliminating all other possibilities, Dupin fixed on the window as the means of entry and egress, and duly found a spring fastening which gave the false impression that the window was nailed down. Since no human could have jumped from the lightning-rod to the window, an ape swinging on the shutter was the only conceivable answer, and a sailor's pigtail-ribbon at the foot of the rod suggested the profession of the owner who must have been hotly pursuing the beast. Further corroboration is provided by a piece of orange fur discovered at the scene, and the inability of the witnesses to identify the language of one of the voices heard arguing.

So far, so watertight. Purists might, however, argue that the narrator – and hence the reader – is offered many crucial pieces of evidence only after the major revelation, or only a few moments before it: the 'puzzle' rule whereby we can be accused of having seen all the evidence but missed its significance is not yet completely in place, though the rhetoric for it is, and directed in equal measure at the clueless narrator and the would-be 'ingenious' but imaginatively hidebound prefect of police.

As well as inventing the detective story (which he called the 'tale of ratiocination'), Poe also invented the single-hero-series form which would become a major element in the subsequent genre. While the second Dupin story 'The Mystery of Marie Rogêt' (an attempt to solve a real-life case before all the evidence was in) is a relative failure, the third and last, 'The Purloined Letter', builds convincingly on the strengths of 'Rue Morgue'. The contrast between Dupin's truly imaginative powers of analysis and the police prefect's plodding ingenuity is now embodied in the whole structure of the story rather than a lengthy introduction and a few sarcastic asides; the main 'secret' of the stolen letter's whereabouts *is* just about deducible by us from the narrated circumstances before Dupin reveals how he deduced it from the same information; even Dupin's gothically eccentric habit of shunning the daylight is now functionally streamlined in his use of pipe-smoke and dark glasses to conceal his own perceptions from those of others. In the suave blackmailer Minister D–, the story also adds to the genre's growing repertoire of motifs the figure of the villain-genius, unlike his orang-utan predecessor an antagonist worthy (or nearly so) of the exalted powers of the detective himself.

Apart from his reported excursion to ascertain what he already knows, Dupin also virtually solves the whole case from his armchair, at a single sitting, while the prefect outlines the problem. This continues a key element of the earlier 'Marie Rogêt', where he cracks the case entirely through an armchair analysis of newspaper reports, and chimes in with the kind of intensity of readerly attention 'at a sitting' Poe elsewhere prescribes for true literary effect.[3]

The novelty and success of Poe's detective short stories depend very much on the fact that they *are* short, designed to be read 'at a sitting' in the popular yet literary-minded periodicals to which Poe devoted much of his creative life. The theory enunciated in 'The Philosophy of Composition' that aesthetic interest dissolves in any work requiring more than one sitting is itself probably connected to his experience of writing short, article-length works devoted to preparing the reader for one particular kind of 'effect', and then satisfying it.[4] The 'effect' for which he was best known was that of gothic horror, and it has been argued that 'Rue Morgue' is something of a halfway house between the grisly trappings of gothic and the determined rationalism of a form better suited to an age of science. In the story's account of a 'double Dupin', whose analytic powers offset a bizarre asociality hinting at an id-like sympathy with the ape, the detective story's not-quite-complete separation from horror is perhaps inscribed. But just as striking is the way in which the Dupin stories seem to celebrate the very act of reading intensely and attentively which they formally demand. By a founding act of deception, 'Rue Morgue' begins not just like but *as* a drily discursive article making the single point that analysis is superior to ingenuity: formally, the rest of the story is provided purely as evidence of this 'scientific' claim, and would lose its purpose if our attention were ever to waver from that fact. The main narrative, likewise, is made to depend on the quality of our attention to an extended newspaper report of the women's murder: essentially, the clues Dupin later finds at the scene are only corroborative of what he has gleaned from that report. If in fact those later clues are rather too plentiful (and too long hidden from us), Poe makes amends in 'Marie Rogêt' by immobilizing Dupin completely in front of a pile of newspaper reports, all of which are quoted in full; and in 'The

Purloined Letter' the prefect's extended narrative of the letter's disappearance allows Dupin to make the crucial deduction, once more, from his armchair.

If that all-important scene of deduction from a single narrative perused in the armchair of a private study can be read as a subliminal advertisement for the short-story form itself, it was not until the 1890s, with Sherlock Holmes, that its endless re-enactment became a fully addictive event. For the intervening half-century, the main developments of the detective form occur in the novel. This means, almost by definition, that they are less 'pure' in their concentration on the single issue of 'who done it': as novels will, they persist in raising a miscellany of other issues – psychological, social and even political.

One of the political shifts particularly registered in nine-teenth-century detective fiction is the emergence of criminal detection itself as a respectable activity. As Ian Ousby and others have argued, the prevailing eighteenth-century attitude to the 'thieftaker' was one of suspicion, and it was not until the establishment by Napoleon in 1812 of the Sûreté, the French criminal investigation department, that the figure of the professional detective began to gain public approval. This was demonstrated most sharply by the immensely successful publication (and instantaneous English translation) in 1829 of the *Mémoires* of François Eugène Vidocq, an ex-criminal who rose to be head of the Sûreté with a trail of daring arrests to his credit. In the same year, Sir Robert Peel founded the Metropolitan Police in London to replace the often corrupt Bow Street Runners, and in 1842 this was augmented by the Detective Police, a department of trained officers soon to be eulogized by Charles Dickens in a series of articles in *Household Words* between 1850 and 1853. In New York, the Day and Night Police were established in 1844, partly in response to the public outcry over the murder of Mary Rogers, lightly fictionalized as Poe's Marie Rogêt. Indeed, this sequence of dates helps to explain why Poe's Dupin stories are set in Paris: though an amateur himself, it is a vital part of the formula that Dupin's brilliance both transcends and is reluctantly endorsed by an existing detective police force as represented by the Prefect G–, to whose predecessor, Vidocq, Dupin explicitly contrasts himself.[5]

It is useful to bear in mind this history of rapidly changing attitudes to detection – both as a newly professionalized police activity and an exciting new set of fantasy possibilities for writers and readers alike – when considering the 'mixed matter' of the nineteenth-century detective novel. One writer who has been unfairly criticized on this score is Emile Gaboriau, whose sequence of novels in the 1860s featuring the detectives Tabaret and Lecoq offers a fascinating exploration of upper- and middle-class hypocrisy in the money-obsessed French Second Empire.[6] The first of these, *L'Affaire Lerouge* (1866), concerns the murder of a retired nursemaid who, it finally turns out, was once involved in an attempt to swap two babies in a way which has secured a noble fortune for one and clerkly drudgery for the other. The amateur detective 'Père' Tabaret, outwardly unimpressive but investigatively streets ahead of the police, deduces rightly from minute clues that the murderer was a gentleman of a certain physical appearance, and for much of the book directs suspicion onto the aristocratic heir, only to discover at the end that the clerkly drudge who claimed to be the victim of the swap was himself the killer, since – though intended by the boys' father – the swap never actually took place. Tabaret's mistake is compounded by his personal fondness for the culprit, with whose mother he is unrequitedly in love.

While even Sherlock Holmes makes mistakes, the novel-length of *Lerouge* protracts Tabaret's error into a major thematic statement, accompanied as it is by many suggestions that he has only turned to detection to sublimate his profound sexual frustration, just as many other characters' social and financial frustrations lead them into crime and other antisocial actions. With the ironic demonstration of his hero's sexual feet of clay – caused in part by a miserly father who forced him to work until too old to marry – Gaboriau finally refocuses the attention that has been absorbed in the thrill of the chase onto the frantic obsession with money and status that seems to have warped all the characters' lives in different ways, and of which the passion for detection is as much a symptom as a cure.

In *Le Crime d'Orcival* (1866), *Le Dossier No. 113* (1867) and *Monsieur Lecoq* (1869), several characters including Tabaret himself reappear, but the leading detective is now the police agent Monsieur Lecoq, who moves from a walk-on role as a reformed criminal to centre-stage as a master of deduction and disguise in the middle two novels, and then with a step back in time to his winning of his detective spurs (criminal past now apparently dropped from the picture) in the last. If this progress expresses a growing confidence on Gaboriau's part in the heroic potential of detection, Lecoq's successes are still often tempered by the realities of a society seen as fundamentally unjust. In the novel bearing his name, Lecoq devotes enormous energy to uncovering the real identity of an uncommunicative prisoner who has murdered some ruffians in a seedy drinking-den. In despair after letting the prisoner escape, Lecoq consults Tabaret and concludes that the prisoner was in fact the Duc de Sairmeuse, a man so powerful that a re-arrest is now unthinkable. In the second half of a very long novel, we are plunged into the background of the murder with only a passing nod to Lecoq's fact-gathering skills: essentially, the book becomes a historical novel about heroic self-sacrifice, revenge and aristocratic skulduggery in the periods of the French Revolution and Restoration, from which the Duc emerges relatively sympathe-tically. His victims in the drinking-den were threatening his wife, whose good name he wished to protect to the end despite her previous murder of the woman he really loved. We have to be content with his absolution on the moral level, since his status places him above the law, although enough of Lecoq's own achievement in the case gets out to ensure his rapid promotion and assured future glory within the force.

In Britain, Gaboriau was probably as big an influence as Poe on Wilkie Collins's novel *The Moonstone*, published in 1868. Here too the leading detective is a policeman, Sergeant Cuff, who not only makes crucial though understandable mistakes, but is also prevented from following the case up thanks to the class difference between himself and the main suspects. In a similar compromise to that in *Monsieur Lecoq*, a last-minute but minor intervention establishes his general brilliance when other narrative assumptions have already gently taken the case out of his hands.

The 'moonstone' of the title is a diamond sent to Rachel Verinder on her eighteenth birthday and stolen from her room on the same night. Her silence about the theft, which makes her Cuff's chief suspect, results from her knowledge that the thief was her cousin and fiancé Franklin Blake – the very man who is most energetic in investigating the case. In a weird dénouement, it turns out that Franklin did indeed remove the diamond, but while unknowingly drugged with opium which made him first hand it to the real villain – another cousin – for safekeeping and then forget the whole incident completely. Crucial in uncovering all this is the social outcast Ezra Jennings, himself an opium addict as was Collins at the time of writing. If the novel has a political theme – and very arguably it does – it is related to its sympathetic treatment of such apparent misfits as Jennings, the deformed maid Rosanna Spearman whose passion for the oblivious Franklin drives her to suicide, and the three incognito brahmins whose single-minded devotion to restoring the diamond to its Indian homeland provides a powerfully anti-imperialist subtext. It is as if the conventional happy ending – the final reunion of Franklin and Rachel – depends on the sacrifice or self-sacrifice of numerous less fortunate victims of social deprivation or persecution, many of whose perspectives we are made to share more or less fully through the fractured, multiple-narrative technique through which the mystery is narrated and unravelled. This fracturing of a simple interest in the case into more complex perspectives is mirrored in the division of the main 'detective' role between the confidently professional (but wrong) Cuff and the marginalized pariah Jennings, enabled to get at the truth through his own experience of illness and addiction.

While other Victorian novels of the 1850s and 1860s – notably Charles Dickens's *Bleak House* and unfinished *The Mystery of Edwin Drood* – contain strong detective elements, these are often overshadowed by an emotional engagement with the criminals which brings them closer to the thriller: some will accordingly be considered in the third chapter. In America, the first whodunnit novel by a woman, Anna K. Green's *The Leavenworth Case* (1878), included a hard-nosed private detective, Ebenezer Gryce, and an apparent revelation of family dysfunction in growing suspicions of the victim's two apparently devoted daughters, the final diversion of which onto a less troubling scapegoat-figure is a common feature of what might be called 'the family whodunnit' from Collins to Christie. In 1886, the runaway success of Fergus Hume's *Mystery of a Hansom Cab* marked a further step in the rise of the whodunnit novel, and also incidentally in the acceptance of Australian fiction in the world market. However, it was with the re-emergence in the 1880s and 1890s of the short-story series formula engineered by Poe, that detective fiction pure and simple took its next great leap forward.

Sir Arthur Conan Doyle's first two novels featuring Sherlock Holmes, *A Study in Scarlet* and *The Sign of Four*, imitated Gaboriau's technique of letting 'pure' detection bring us half-way, then cutting away to a historically specific explanation of the criminal's motives before returning to a present-tense finale again dominated by the detective. Though only moderately successful, these two novels paved the way for the simple but financially brilliant idea Doyle later described thus in his autobiography *Memories and Adventures*: 'It had struck me that a single character running through a series, if it only engaged the attention of the reader, would bind that reader to that particular magazine'.[7]

In 1891 this idea was realized in the transference of Holmes to the short-story series formula in the new *Strand* magazine, whose energetic proprietor George Newnes was on the look-out for just such forward-looking schemes. Appearing monthly in the magazine and then in yearly twelve-story book republications, the Holmes stories rapidly became a sensation. It is debatable, however, how far this was due to something unique in their hero or even their author, and how far to the notion of the series itself, once pushed this far beyond Poe's three haphazardly produced Dupin stories.

The notion of Holmes as a unique or superbly characterized personality is arguably a myth: what is far more interesting about him is the way in which he encapsulates some of the qualities of the series form itself within a fairly loose envelope of potentially contradictory traits. These traits are initially scraped together from Poe's dégagé intellectual joker Dupin, and from Gaboriau's melancholic bachelor Tabaret and ferret-eyed professional Lecoq. From the more energetic, animal-like elements of these characters emerges the brash, anti-intellectual Holmes of *A Study in Scarlet*, whose sneers at Dupin and Lecoq as detectives hold an honourable place in the oedipal predecessor-bashing which is one of the ritual pleasures of series detection.[8] From the more reflective, melancholy sides of the same characters emerges the completely different Holmes of *The Sign of Four*, an intellectual aesthete to his fingertips whose drug-induced fondness for literary quotation and bored distantiation from his friend Watson's gruff heterosexuality may have been influenced by a meeting with Oscar Wilde, whose *The Picture of Dorian Gray* appeared in the same magazine (*Lippincott's*) in 1890.

By various devices, including a repeated leaping back and forth in time to periods before and after the series's one irreversible event – Watson's marriage in *The Sign of Four* – the series proper manages to blend, or blur, these two somewhat different Holmeses into an apparent unity. It might be argued that this 'dual nature' increasingly expresses the tensions within the series form itself. The decisiveness, the refusal of large ideas, the need to get to the point, express the brevity of the short story and the reader's need to emerge with a single apex-like solution to all that has been said and done. On the other hand, the dreaminess, the quest for something ever more 'singular' and *outré*, the growing *ennui* and dread of routine, express the series form's growing ability and urge to reflect on its own repetitiousness. The early story 'The Red Headed League', in which Holmes's 'dual nature' is most explicitly discussed, is also the one where many images of repetition and urban reproducibility are offset with the ability of two individuals – Holmes and the criminal genius John Clay – to think beyond and through these, to great comic effect. The fantastic newspaper ad attracting red-headed men from all quarters of London, the pointless labour of writing out the *Encyclopaedia Britannica* from A to Z, the 'manufactory of artificial kneecaps' where the crooks' trail runs cold, are offset with the knowledge of real underlying connections which make all these absurd phenomena useful and interpretable to the criminal digger beneath walls and the detective reader of the knees of trousers. This awareness of the dance between reproducibility and uniqueness is, arguably, what makes 'Sherlock Holmes' tick, both as a series and as a character.

In terms of content, certain situations recur repeatedly throughout the fifty-six stories and four novels comprising the complete Holmes canon. The most common of these concerns a foreign secret society, engaged in a battle to the death with an absconding ex-member who is usually its victim but sometimes a scourge avenging its previous victims. In a frequent variant of this situation, the society is replaced by a conspiracy of silence surrounding a crime committed in the British colonies or in America, the ensuing struggle being between those who have built a new, respectable life with the proceeds of the crime and those who return to claim their share of it. In a further variant, the conspiracy becomes a secret marriage or betrothal (again colonial or American), and the returnee the husband or lover reclaiming his wife or fiancée from a 'respectable' British marriage. Despite their shared theme of foreign threats to outwardly stable British households, these three types of situation are treated in strikingly different ways: the secret-society struggles tend to play themselves out tragically but then retire from Britain for good, despite much (often strangely ineffectual) code-deciphering by Holmes;[9] the wealth and respectability bought by colonial conspirators tends to be handed down, often to their daughters, with Holmes helping to draw a veil over its source;[10] and the love-affair from the rough-and-ready past tends to be applauded and helped on by Holmes, in stories challenging the false notions of 'respectability' which have threatened it.[11]

Elsewhere in the canon, individual villains come in several recurrent shapes, of which the most vicious is the impoverished member of the rural squirearchy desperate to inherit or hold on to an estate by murdering or imprisoning its rightful beneficiaries.[12] Professional working-class criminals are very few, but servants sometimes make one-off bids for their betters' property:[13] both these and the savage squires tend to be destroyed by the very means with which they plan to commit their crimes. The higher aristocracy are generally only threatened by disgrace, from which Holmes duly saves them with an icy personal contempt.[14] By contrast to other classes, hard-working middle-class professionals are very unlikely to be criminals, though some of the most interesting stories deal with the extraordinary lengths to which members of the aspiring lower-middle classes can go to conceal their financial difficulties without actually committing any crime. In several such stories, women are the prime objects of deception, as they often are of the savage squires' more murderous attempts: as a general rule, Holmes tries hard to protect women from any knowledge of the skulduggery of which their menfolk are capable.[15] One or two independent-minded women are applauded,[16] but when women do commit crimes it is almost always at the instigation of men on whom they are emotionally dependent.[17]

Simply by virtue of its inevitable repetitiousness, the sixty-story Holmes canon provides an interesting X-ray of the range of social attitudes to which it must have appealed: fear of serious organized crime as a largely foreign infection, to be repelled whenever possible from our shores; awareness that the rough trade of empire-building may provide a conduit for such infection, balanced with a grudging respect for its contribution to the nation's fortunes; suspicion of the older, feudal and rural, classes by contrast to the hardworking urban middle class; fitful awareness of the suppression of women's freedom within the traditional family structure, coupled with reluctance to challenge that structure itself.

Between Holmes's heyday of the 1890s and the end of World War I, the whodunnit entered what might be called its Age of Spoofery. With the success of the formula so clearly established by Doyle, many other writers with other literary goals ultimately in mind 'tried their hands' at the genre while clearly also wishing to comment self-reflexively on it. Several of these are clearly in touch with the agendas of socialism and/or what has come to be called modernism. Hence, in the work of writers such as Arthur Morrison, Israel Zangwill, G. K. Chesterton and E. C. Bentley, genre-based expectations are deliberately set up, only to be shattered by solutions in which the detectives are mistaken or guilty in ways which suggest that we, the popular readership, are all too willing to be taken for a ride by superman fantasies as a substitute for confronting society's real problems.

Hence, as well as writing the straightforwardly Holmesian Martin Hewitt series, the socialist Arthur Morrison also created Dorrington, a private detective who in case after case unscrupulously robs, blackmails or even murders his way to whatever loot is in the offing, blithely repeating his view that, in a world of ruthless capitalist competition, 'Everybody does it'.[18] Another socialist, Israel Zangwill, produced in the one-off short novel *The Big Bow Mystery* (1892) a story in which the great detective Grodman galvanizes the newspaper-reading public into a frenzied competition to solve the 'locked-room' murder he has been called in on, only to reveal that he did it himself, purely to add one last great case to the forthcoming publication of his achievements. The fact that the victim was an active socialist of outstanding virtue underscores the point that, in being hoodwinked into looking the wrong way by the detective cult, the public are overlooking the only real source of social solutions. Still with a (somewhat vaguer) anti-capitalist agenda in mind, E. C. Bentley's *Trent's Last Case* (1913) presents a more sympathetic detective who is, nonetheless, comprehensively mistaken in his solution of the murder of the capitalist Sigsbee Manderson, a man so unpleasant that we feel he deserved to die anyway. Bentley's friend G. K. Chesterton created numerous detective series, of which the Father Brown stories are only the most famous. In the first few of these (*The Innocence of Father Brown*, 1911), our expectations are repeatedly toyed with as the apparent detective-hero of the first, Valentin, becomes the surprise culprit of the second, while Flambeau, the master-criminal bested by Father Brown in several stories, later becomes his faithful ally and 'Watson'. While excited by the populist 'romance' of the detective form,[19] Chesterton repeatedly uses it as a kind of object-lesson in abandoning unthinking assumptions and prejudices (though he sometimes replaces them with even less palatable ones of his own, as in the antisemitic 1922 collection, *The Man Who Knew Too Much*).

In France, too, an element of self-reflexive spoofery was in the air. Less dangerously than Dorrington but more so than A. W. Hornung's Raffles (1899), Maurice Leblanc's Arsène Lupin repeatedly uses all the ingenuity of detection to defy the law, at one point outwitting the great 'Holmlock Shears' himself. In Gaston Leroux's novel *Le Mystère de la chambre jaune* (1907), the apparent great detective turns out to be the murderer, but also – in a riot of oedipal implications – the father of the boy-detective hero Rouletabille, whose mother was the victim. Despite its potentially traumatic content (and Freud's ideas might have just about reached Leroux in 1907), the novel's drily humorous tone and commitment to the minutiae of its country-house setting (including a map) were a particular influence on the consolidator of what may be seen as the next major phase of British detective writing: Agatha Christie.

2

The Detective Whodunnit from Christie to the Present

Arguably, the prewar impulse to comment explicitly on the genre's essential artificiality, and to mix it up with other kinds of moral, emotional and political concern, had to die down before an acceptably stable way of transmuting the strengths of the Holmes-like short story into the novel could be found. Hence, despite many partial precedents, it was only after the First World War that the British whodunnit novel came fully into its own. With *The Mysterious Affair at Styles* (1920), Agatha Christie established a pattern of extraordinary resilience. A murder during a gathering at a country house provides enough intertwined characters with enough possible motives to fill a novel, albeit a short one, needing little else to keep it going by way of change of scene or much elaboration of character. A few outside forays apart, the action and *dramatis personae* are as it were frozen in time and place by the murder, as in a snapshot, allowing a picture of a single social group, 'typical' even if in crisis, to develop slowly and with satisfying completeness.

While the book's detective, Hercule Poirot, also proved highly resilient, his character is less crucial to the overall effect than the pattern of shifting suspicion by which the case is unravelled. It is, however, important that he is a thoroughly respectable figure, able to call on police support despite some occasional shortlived mockery, and not personally involved with any of the suspects beyond a broad concern to avoid unnecessary scandal about the generally upper-middle-class society they represent. While all these traits can be found at times in Holmes, Poirot and his many successors are far less wildly impressive figures: indeed, the device most often used to differentiate them from their more demonic precursors is an apparently ineffectual or even buffoonish exterior, represented in Poirot's case by his short stature, baldness, physical pernicketiness and inescapable foreignness. (While traditional British attitudes could be relied on to regard a French accent as inherently absurd, the role of 'gallant little Belgium' in the recent Great War added a more positive element, as perhaps did Christie's own early enthusiasm for French detective fiction such as Leroux's.)

With the Christie-style whodunnit, the emphasis shifts from the brilliant detective's following-up of clues through a range of territories, to the successive investigation of the stories and half-truths of a reasonably large group of suspects, immobilized in place and, effectively, in time. To maintain our interest in them, it is important that each suspect should have, or appear to have, 'something to hide': usually a less important crime, an unacknowledged sexual or other relationship, a desire to protect another party, or some other private obsession.[1] While forfeiting the reader's primary interest once revealed, these minor by-plots provide much of the books' 'novelish' material, as well as the camouflaging undergrowth within which the apparently least likely suspect can be revealed as the murderer. Rightly praised as the past-mistress of this technique, Christie began in *Styles* as she was often later to go on, with the striking double-bluff of offering a 'most-likely' suspect whom the reader is bound to reject from the start, but who nonetheless emerges as the real culprit.

With *The Murder of Roger Ackroyd* (1926), the 'least-likely' game took a step forward which, for some critics, threatened the whole basis of the genre by breaking one of its most cardinal rules: that the narration itself should be free from suspicion. In the tradition of Poe and Doyle, the narrator was often a 'Watson', a loyal friend of the detective whose narration was supposedly just a transparent rendition of his (and by implication the reader's) obtuseness in the face of evidence whose real significance the detective grasped but did not explain until the end. In *Styles* and other early novels, Christie provided Poirot with just such a Watson, the dim but game Captain Hastings. Though in *Ackroyd* Poirot repeatedly bemoans Hastings's absence, his role is apparently taken over by the well-liked Doctor Sheppard, who as Poirot's next-door neighbour and a trusted figure in the village of King's Abbott, takes to accompanying Poirot on his investigations while – as he carefully explains to us – writing up the narrative we are actually reading, in the hope of clarifying the case by recording every significant detail from before the murder to the present. This helpful function is underlined when, three-quarters of the way through, he actually hands Poirot the whole narration so far, writing the rest of it at a moment only indicated at the very end. That moment turns out to be the last few hours before his suicide, his innocent-sounding narration having only confirmed Poirot's suspicions that he is the murderer. One of the book's most memorable features is the quiet writerly pride with which the doomed Sheppard directs our attention to the ambiguities and partial omissions by which he presented the moment of the murder as a polite and considerate farewell to a still-living friend whom all the evidence (rigged by Sheppard himself) indicated as having been killed much later.

While some critics at the time disapproved of *Ackroyd*'s supposed removal of the reader's access to trustworthy evidence, Christie takes great care not to let Sheppard actually lie to us at any point: it is only by what he does not say, and our genre-based expectations of his Watson-like role, that we are deceived. Once that deception is removed, the whole book has to be reread (or at least mentally recapitulated, following the promptings of Christie/Sheppard) in a new light: not only the key moment but many others turn out to have been highly ironic or ambiguous, and the apparent lack of any but the flattest style emerges as in itself a stylistic feat of great ingenuity. In this, as in some contemporaneous modernist works, the novel works interestingly as a critique of the narrative function in fiction more generally: with the collapse of the 'reliable narrator', other assumptions about literature as a mouthpiece of univocal authority can also be felt to crumble.

Despite such moments of formal innovation, the social vision of Christie's novels is, famously, very conservative.[2] Country houses and/or upper-middle-class village communities may provide the satisfyingly manageable closed societies demanded by the form; they also purvey a typifying vision of British Society as a whole strikingly at odds with many insistent realities of the interwar years, from the devastation of the Great War to the

21

mass unemployment and depression of the 1920s and 1930s. As a woman who had herself found a degree of independence, as a wartime hospital worker and then as a highly successful writer, Christie might at least have been expected to celebrate the increase in women's rights accompanying the Female Suffrage of 1928. Such 'celebration' (if it was that) was, however, somewhat slow and sidelong in coming: only in 1930, with *The Murder at the Vicarage*, did the type of gossipy village spinster-with-nothing-better-to-do satirized in the figure of Dr Sheppard's sister Caroline appear as an amateur detective in her own right, in the figure of Miss Marple. Emerging rather slowly from a chorus of similar old gossips, Miss Marple powerfully embodies the quietist notion that no special training or empowerment is necessary for women's traditionally allowed gift for 'snooping' into their neighbours' affairs to be transformed into the social usefulness symbolically conferred by the role of 'great detective'. Unlike the militant detective heroines of more recent fiction (but also unlike such nineteenth-century forebears as Loveday Brooke and Lady Molly of Scotland Yard),[3] Miss Marple is no private eye battling against masculinist assumptions about her job, nor a policewoman fighting her way tooth and nail up the ranks. She is simply an incarnation of upper-middle-class English village life at its most apparently insular and inward-turned.

That is how she began, anyway: since St Mary Mead could hardly be expected to produce a sufficient yield of murders on a regular basis, with her success it became necessary to move her on to a succession of other similar villages, either at the grudging behest of the police or on visits to friends or relations. In the later *A Murder is Announced* (1950), such a visit works effectively to bring out some of the changes in Christie's view of the village as a microcosm of society at large. While working on her regular assumption that the whole world of human motivation is indeed summed up in her knowledge of St Mary Mead, Miss Marple does also register a changed world where hardly anything in the endearingly named village of Chipping Cleghorn is as it seems. The traditional big house, Dyas Hall, has 'suffered during the war years'[4] and is now overgrown with weeds; at the other large house, Little Paddocks, the apparently thriving household consists largely of recent arrivals doubtful as to each others' real identities – a situation reflected throughout the village as a whole, however outwardly reassuring its traditional gallery of retired colonels, fluffy-minded widows and comically over-erudite vicars. The eponymous murder and a string of others turn out to be committed by the apparent linchpin of this society, who has only appeared in it well after the war during which she is thought to have made her fortune, though in fact she is only impersonating a sister whom no one else has ever met. Though such deceptions are of course common in Christie and throughout the genre, the impact of the Second World War in shattering any remaining sense of organic, long-established community is dwelt on throughout the book, from the main plot to the portrayal of the paranoid refugee cook Mitzi, whose dread of secret police and concentration camps is a source of much routinely xenophobic but unpleasantly insensitive comedy.

Many of the assumptions and formal techniques found in Christie can also be found in other writers of 'classic' whodunnits; and in a study of this brevity it will not be possible to consider them in even comparable depth. Dorothy Sayers, Margery Allingham, Ngaio Marsh and Michael Innes, who all began work in the later 1920s or early 1930s, owe many debts to Christie while all aiming at a slightly more intellectual audience. Though their detectives remain likeable rather than imposing, they are more establishment 'insider' figures than the oddballs Poirot and Miss Marple: Sayers's Lord Peter Wimsey is a lord who knows all the right people and just happens to detect, while Allingham's Albert Campion, Marsh's Roderick Alleyn and Innes's John Appleby are all almost equally upper-class figures who just happen to be policemen (though Campion's precise position remains tantalizingly undefined). Far from being lonely eccentrics, all four inhabit solid networks of mutually supportive relationships – with wives, extended families, trusty manservants and police colleagues – which develop throughout their respective series in ways which continuously affirm their personal stake in the social order they work to protect. The effortless social ease of these detectives is further bolstered by an intellectual insiderliness expressed partly through the conscious stylishness of the writing, and partly through the detectives' own easy way with a quotation: in Allingham and Innes particularly, a highbrow literary reference is likelier to encode the mystery than one of the nursery rhymes favoured by Christie in *Ten Little Niggers, One, Two, Buckle My Shoe* or *A Pocketful of Rye*.

It would thus be fair to generalize that these detectives are very complete fantasy-projections of a readership anxious to believe that an establishment led by such well-bred, well-educated men could still be trusted to protect a threatened and divided British society from itself. Men: the three women among these authors all remained loyal to the male detectives with whom they built their reputations, even though they all eventually provided them with scholarly or artistic wives through whose sensitively observant eyes the build-ups to the deductive climaxes are increasingly seen. This is not to say that these books are uniformly reactionary: once the rightness of the central subject-position is accepted, various psychological and social issues can be explored with considerable sharpness. Sayers's *Gaudy Night* (1935) directs detection towards an examination of the still-active debate over women's place in, and right to, higher education. Innes's *Lament for a Maker* (1938) builds up an impressive picture of Anglo-Scottish and class relationships in a multivocal form like that of Collins's *The Moonstone*, before collapsing into near farce at the end (a common failing with this writer). Marsh's late *Black as He's Painted* (1974) explores colour prejudice from an angle whose liberal intentions are precisely conveyed in one of the punning titles at which Marsh is particularly adept. Margery Allingham's *The Tiger in the Smoke* (1952) deliberately juxtaposes Campion's upper-class world with that of a working-class criminal gang whose lives have been irrevocably warped by the Second World War, from which the country as a whole is seen to be only painfully recovering. The wider sense of a shattering of shared values is mirrored in a fracturing of the book's form, in which the traditional detective imperatives of the whodunnit are overshadowed by a thriller-like absorption in the career of the gang's psychopathic leader Jack Havoc, a rough beast slouching energetically towards the Bethlehem of postwar welfare-state Britain.

Other significant writers to emerge between the wars include: Anthony Berkeley, whose spoof-like *The Poisoned Chocolates Case* (1929) pulls a series of brilliant tricks on the reader in the tradition of Bentley's *Trent's Last Case*; Josephine Tey, whose highly individual books from *The Man in the Queue* (also 1929) onwards cannot be categorized in terms of any single type of whodunnit despite the occasional appearance of the same detective; and Nicholas Blake (a pseudonym of the poet C. Day Lewis from 1935), whose police detective Nigel Strangeways hints at left-wing views while representing much the same mix of social positions as Alleyn or Appleby.

The establishment unassumingness of most British interwar detectives can to some extent be contrasted with the greater flamboyance of American whodunnit protagonists in the same period: from 1926, S. S. Van Dine's Philo Vance (who according to Ogden Nash 'Needs a kick in the pance')[5] flaunts his Oxford education and quasi-aristocratic mannerisms in ways which, in an American context, constitute a form of aggression rather than social camouflage; Rex Stout's overweight, orchid-fancying Nero Wolfe (1934) follows on from Dupin or Holmes as larger-than-life eccentric genius, his refusal ever to leave his house ensuring endless bravura displays of armchair deduction as well as a nod to less hothouse detective forms in his verbal sparrings with his private-eye-like agent Archie Goodwin. Though setting his books chiefly in Britain, John Dickson Carr resembles his fellow American Stout in a career-long embrace of a specific restriction (all his cases are variants of the 'locked room' mystery) and preference for a flamboyantly characterized detective, Dr Gideon Fell (apparently modelled on G. K. Chesterton). Though Wolfe is of European (Montenegrin) stock rather than British, he, Vance and Fell represent a significantly American interwar 'take' on a kind of Old World culture combining eccentric individualism with tightly formal self-restriction, which is still seen as impressive rather than modestly normative.

After the Second World War, the whodunnit's survival seemed for a while dependent on the strikingly long productive careers of most of the writers discussed above. While Sayers wrote her last detective novel in 1937, most of her contemporaries continued writing them almost until their deaths: Tey's in 1952, Allingham's in 1966, Berkeley's in 1971, Blake/Day Lewis's in 1972, Christie's in 1976, Carr's in 1977 and Marsh's in 1982. By the 1960s, as new 'realistic' influences from America and television took prominence and the prewar generation gradually fell silent, it was

25

possible to argue that the British-style whodunnit they had created was on the wane for good.

By the 1970s, however, new reputations were being consolidated by writers who seemed to have discovered new ways of grafting contemporary realistic observation onto the old form. Gone, first of all, were the aristocratic trappings of some predecessors: the series detectives of Colin Watson, Peter Dickinson, P. D. James, Ruth Rendell and Reginald Hill are simply hard-working professional policemen. Gone too, often, were the stately homes and idyllic villages: the settings of murder were now more often quietly domestic or the semi-public, shared spaces of welfare-state Britain.

For the most celebrated of these writers, P. D. (now Baroness) James, there are in fact very clear substitutes for the elements that 'upper-classness' might have been felt to entail before the war. First, there is culture: her series-hero Dalgleish may be a policeman but he is also a published poet, a glimpse of one of whose slim volumes on a suspect's bookshelf is, like other forms of instantly grasped literary allusion, enough to establish their credentials as enlightened and sensitive, if not necessarily innocent. Second, though the settings are often semi-public workplaces, many of these (a forensic laboratory, a teaching hospital, a nursing home, a publishing house) are actually awkwardly converted from prewar stately homes, as in the training hospital in *Shroud for a Nightingale* (1973), where 'the iron staples, driven brutally into the woodwork...were in incongruous contrast to the row of elegant light fittings',[6] or the publishing house in *Original Sin* (1995) where the dining room of a Venetian-style palazzo has been equally brutally divided in half. If life in egalitarian Britain is there to be got on with, James implies, we don't necessarily have to like it. Much the same seems to be implied in her insistent but unenthralled presentation of that modern invention, sex, a certain distaste for which is also conveyed in Dalgleish's personal solitude: long-divorced, his only real relationships are professional ones. In later novels, the most important of these has been with Kate Miskin, an ambitious working-class police detective whose struggles to balance a difficult home background with her job make her a welcome if somewhat belated replacement for Cordelia Gray, the feminist heroine of James's groundbreaking 1972 private-eye novel *An Unsuitable Job for a Woman* (to be discussed later).

Whereas Dalgleish has followed such predecessors as Innes's Appleby (and perhaps his creator) in a series of promotions higher and higher up the social scale, the patrolling of a relatively localized beat is a feature of most other police series-heroes in recent decades. Many such beats – the Flaxborough of Colin Watson's Inspector Purbright, the Kingsmarkham of Ruth Rendell's Inspector Wexford or the Oxford of Colin Dexter's Inspector Morse – have been real or fictional smallish towns in contemporary Britain. For most TV police series too, from Z *Cars* in the 1960s onwards, such localism has been a key element in turning attention away from the well-heeled closed society and eccentrically brilliant detective towards a more 'realistic' notion of crime as something that happens every day, arising from the pressures of a common life. Even where the setting is foreign-yet-familiar as befits a post-1960s postcolonial, touristic and televisual culture (the Bombay of H. R. F. Keating's Inspector Ghote, the Amsterdam of Nicholas Freeling's Van der Valk, the Venice of Michael Dibdin's Aurelio Zen), the sense of crime as endemic but ultimately assuageable by benignly professional police 'procedure' prevails. If one apparent revolt from such police heroes back towards the 'inspired amateur' school has been Ellis Peters's Brother Cadfael series, set in medieval Shrewsbury and featuring a monk as detective, even here the social role of the monastery, as a natural place for those in trouble to turn to, makes it a persuasive – if very nostalgic – image of an authority able to solve a local community's problems on a repeated basis.

An image of benignly paternalist British policing also underlies one of the most assured recent developments of the classic whodunnit mode, Elizabeth George's Inspector Lynley series. Like John Dickson Carr, however, George is an American writing about Britain, and the cultural distance this involves allows her to draw on aspects of the traditional whodunnit few contemporary British writers would be willing or able to handle with a straight face. Thus, as well as being a police inspector, her main detective, Thomas Lynley, also happens to be the eighth Earl of Asherton, and his two inseparable companions on most cases are the almost equally top-drawer forensic scientist Simon Allcourt-St James and his occasional assistant Lady Helen Clyde, with whom Lynley is unrequitedly in love and who was once also involved with St James. Preposterous though this scenario is, George comes close to making it believable, though the amount of time expended on the emotional contortions of the trio helps to account for the increasingly unwieldy length of the later novels.

One element that helps to counteract the Wimseyesque datedness of this scenario is the inclusion of the working-class Sergeant Barbara Havers as the fourth member of the series-team. Closely modelled as she may be on P. D. James's Kate Miskin, Havers forcibly articulates her (and hence potentially our) hatred of the British class system at every turn while, of course, always remaining loyal to Lynley as a human being and a good policeman. Lynley's own position in the class system, once accepted, is also often played against the grain: no one hates the special privileges it throws his way more than he – he is just trying to do his job.

In the second novel of the series, *Payment in Blood* (1989), all these *données* are skilfully worked into a conventional country-house murder plot such as – again – few British writers would be willing to handle. Though the country house has just become a hotel, it is also the home of the aristocratic family of Lord Stinhurst, now involved – in another highly traditional ploy – in theatrical preparations for a major West End opening. The murder of the play's author, Joy Sinclair, is complicated for Lynley by two factors: the presence of Lady Helen, apparently in bed with the play's director in the only room with access to the victim's, and the fact that his class seems to have played a part in getting him deputed to a case involving another lord: a point to which Havers draws much ferocious attention. Against formulaic expectations, Lynley turns out to be wrong almost all down the line, precisely because of these emotionally compli-cating factors. He believes Lord Stinhurst's initial cover story almost unquestioningly on the word of a gentleman, and was given the case on precisely this expectation by an MI5 anxious to conceal the fact that Stinhurst's brother was murdered by his father as a Russian spy. At the same time, Lynley's obsession with Lady Helen convinces him that her current lover murdered the playwright and, though his investigations uncover the crucial motive, it turns out to apply to a different, barely suspected, member of the theatrical group. By contrast, Sergeant Havers is almost completely right: though her own class-prejudices lead her to fix on Stinhurst for the present murder, he is indeed guilty of a great deal; and her awareness of Lynley's emotional fixation convinces her, well before him, of the innocence of Lady Helen's lover.

This honourable division of spoils between Lynley – who does finally catch the real killer and denounce his MI5 puppetmasters – and Havers expresses the real ambivalence in George's fiction between the deeply comforting fantasy of a stable traditional order for which many Americans still look to Britain, and a sharp awareness of the inadequacy of that order from many contemporary and indeed democratic perspectives. There is a similar ambivalence in her approach to plot. On the one hand, there is a sense of too much of a good thing in the 'closed society' possibilities offered by a bickering theatrical company, within an isolated and snowbound hotel (shades of Christie's *The Mousetrap* here), which is also the ancestral family home of a good half of the suspects. This sense of overload is also present in the excess of aristocratic and over-significantly named detectives: Lynley evoking the one member of the British royal family widely known to have taken an ordinary job (the Queen's nephew Viscount Linley), and Allcourt-St James calling to mind 'the court of St James', to which American ambassadors are famously appointed. On the other hand, the traditional *mise-en-scène* is there to be taken apart in fairly radical ways: not only is the detective mistaken, but he is so because the British establishment has cynically used his most precious asset – his breeding – against him. He is also mistaken because one of the most basic rules of the classic whodunnit – the detective's non-involvement with the suspects – has been broken right from the start and twice over in his and his trusted partner's past and present relationships with the prime suspect, Lady Helen. In the novel's structure there is a deliberate sense of forcing new wine into old bottles, and waiting for them to explode.

In America, the police procedural has developed more of its own dynamic away from the paternalist conventions of the whodunnit than in Britain. Starting with Ed McBain's 87th Precinct novels in the 1960s, the American procedural usually expresses almost as much interest in the way a team of professionals, with various problems of their own, work together as in the solutions of crimes. Normally – and this is where George's mixture feels somewhat anomalous – the crimes presented in procedurals are multiple rather than single: for McBain's Steve Carella and his associates, several major investigations are on the go concurrently, and the 'win some, lose some' formula this enables allows a welcome new level of realism into the genre. In a common more recent development, the notion of multiple criminality is, as it were, stylized into the shape of a single criminal whose activities are sufficiently threatening to tie up convincingly the resources of a procedural-type team: the serial killer. Often this move is accompanied by a corresponding stylization of the team ethos around a single protagonist who is emphatically working with the police, but whose struggle for personal validation is particularly strongly tied up with the professional struggle against the killer who sums up all the horror and apparent randomness of the violence lurking somewhere 'out there'.

From such constructions (arguably) has arisen a split-level formula very specific to the 1980s and 1990s. In this formula, we follow for some time the actions of a professional investigator (whether from the police or its legal, forensic or 'psychological profiling' adjuncts), including the way the actions of a serial murderer increase the strain on that investigator's life and feelings. As the investigator starts to make headway with the case, however, the pure 'detective' interest starts to give way to a narrative of the killer's activities which makes stopping him or her the reader's overriding concern until the point where the hero(ine) finally manages to do so. In novels such as Elmore Leonard's *City Primeval* (1980), *Split Images* (1981) and *Glitz* (1985), where we are introduced to the killer's thoughts and feelings early on, the final confrontation often carries some explicit or implicit reference to the showdown in the kind of Westerns Leonard began his career by writing, owing its power to the unnerving evenhandedness with which the bad guy is shown to have just as rich a personality and sense of style as the good guy. In Robert Harris's *The Silence of the Lambs* (1989), our focus on the policewoman Clarice's investigation is similarly cut short somewhat later in the day by a direct narration of the killer's thoughts and actions, and if these are too bizarre to be very convincing, the sense of an intensely personal duel is established from the start by the introduction of the more compelling Dr Hannibal Lecter, himself a serial killer who is also the heroine's chief mentor as to the killer's psychological 'profile'.

One of the procedural genre's most currently successful practitioners is Patricia Cornwell, most of whose novels begin with a murder bearing all the hallmarks of a known serial killer and then follow the case up through the eyes of Kay Scarpetta, the Chief Medical Examiner of Richmond, Virginia, whose forensic expertise makes her a leading figure in the subsequent investigation. While the first-person narration ensures a more singleminded focus on detection than the 'split-level' form described above, the killer is a constant, active presence throughout all Cornwell's books (and sometimes introduced to us more directly in brief flashes of italicized description or interior monologue). So insistent has the formulaic need for a serial killer to fuel the right responses from the reader become, however, that, as the series has progressed, the more localized murders of individual books have been overarched by the duel with Kay initiated by a kind of meta-serial killer (or *series* killer), Temple Gault, who seemed to be becoming as firm a fixture as Kay's trusted collaborators Pete Marino and Benton Wesley until finally killed off in the seventh novel, *From Potter's Field* (1995).

Her first novel, *Postmortem* (1990, written before her formula's unassuageable hunger for serial killers fresh or stale had become so evident), is a good example of the way in which the contemporary procedural uses classic whodunnit procedures to identify a criminal who is no longer 'in here' – one of a closed circle of known suspects – but 'out there' – identifiable only through the gradual narrowing-down of possibilities which potentially include the whole society. In a class I taught recently, some students found the final confrontation with a police telephone operator we had never met or heard named before unfair, but the point is that his job (as well as an appropriately scapegoating disability in the shape of a tell-tale body odour) eventually makes him the one person in the city the killer could conceivably be. What the novel also exemplifies well is a current interest in 'psychological profiling', the quasi-magical projection of the criminal's personality and likely future actions from an expert ability to read the signs left by their previous crimes.

Here this role of psychologist-guru is played by the FBI man Benton Wesley (subsequently Kay's main love-interest); in *The Silence of the Lambs* it is taken, weirdly, by the Dr Lecter who adds unparalleled psychological expertise to his own penchant for murder and cannibalism; in the powerful British TV series *Cracker* it is (or was) taken by the flawed hero Fitz, whose inability to sort out his own life in no way detracts from his almost saviour-like powers once he is on a case.

Though there may be a hankering for a return to the shamanic Holmesian superman in such figures, able to reassure us that somewhere there is a science from which even the anonymity of the modern city offers no shelter, *Postmortem* and most of the other procedural texts discussed in the last few pages strongly celebrate teamwork. Partly, this has to do with realism: few major crimes are in fact solved by solitary individuals these days, or were perhaps ever. But it is also perhaps connected with an image of social integration which seems under threat elsewhere: in dovetailing numerous skills, interests and preoccupations (including those of the reader) towards the knitting up of a constantly unravelling society, the police whodunnit perhaps expresses the fact that for many people the fullest sense of community now on offer is to be found in the world of work.

In several of the texts just considered, this sense of social validation through work is particularly highlighted in the case of women protagonists. The validation is that much more intense when – as in *Postmortem* and *The Silence of the Lambs* – the killer to be tracked down is specifically a man killing women for sexual reasons. In a form which gives welcome scope for women to escape the domestic sphere to which many other fictional genres might still tend to assign them, the male serial-killer scenario also gives full scope for a powerful communication of solidarity and identification with other women. At the same time, the teamwork ethos allows for a carefully nuanced calibration of where the struggle for gender equality in the workplace has got to at any given moment, with a spectrum across the team from blatant sexism to full co-operation, with one or more characters (e.g. Cornwell's Pete Marino) sliding from the former to the latter as the narrative proceeds.

For this and the other reasons stated above, the serial-killer formula seems almost to have become a fixture. One danger of this situation for the genre is that it is ultimately a blind alley: with only one type of crime on the agenda, the possible new permutations are likely to become increasingly limited. Another danger is that such narratives come to be read as accurately reflecting an unstoppable trend in 'real' crime, so that the fiction-led mass-fear of the serial murderer becomes the lens through which attitudes to actual debates about crime and punishment are shaped – usually in the illiberal directions indicated in the demand by the former British Prime Minister John Major that society as a whole should learn to 'condemn a little more, and understand a little less'.

3

The *Noir* Thriller

The thriller, where the action is primarily in the present tense and the protagonists are threatened by powerful forces of some kind, has two distinct branches. First, there is the *noir* thriller, where we identify with protagonists who consciously exceed the law. This group extends from classical tragedy to ambivalent celebrations of criminal milieux to more individualized studies of transgression. Second, there is the anti-conspiracy thriller, where the protagonists confront a powerful conspiracy of wrongdoers without the guaranteed support of the forces of law and order. This group includes most spy fiction as well as much adventure fiction in which heroes match their powers against villains, and will be discussed in the next chapter.

The narrative which follows the exploits of a criminal in the present tense goes back at least to such tragedies as *Richard III* and *Macbeth,* and such early novels as Defoe's *Moll Flanders, Colonel Jack* and *Roxana.* Defoe's novels themselves rise out of an eighteenth-century culture with a highly ambiguous attitude to crime, where on the one hand public executions and the criminals' penitent confession of wrongdoing were aspects of popular entertainment, but on the other hand the same criminals were often perceived as heroes, especially under a penal code so savagely sweeping yet inefficient that 'there but for the grace of God go I' must have been a very common feeling. Defoe's sometimes bewildering mixture of understanding and condemnation towards his protagonists is also evident in his reporting of the lives of such real-life criminals as Jack Sheppard and Jonathan Wild, two figures who remained the star-turns of the various compilations of criminal lives known collectively as *The Newgate Calendar.*[1]

A century later, in the 1830s, novelists such as Harrison

Ainsworth and Edward Bulwer-Lytton shaped such ambivalent feelings, and much of the same material, into a semi-fictionalized form recognizably similar to the modern thriller: the Newgate novel. Ainsworth's *Jack Sheppard: A Romance of the Robber-Hero* (1839) mixes a somewhat conventional romance-plot, hinging on noble birthrights and long-lost cousins, with painstakingly researched accounts of the exploits of the housebreaker Jack Sheppard and his nemesis, the thieftaker-gangster Jonathan Wild. If the romance-plot demands that Jack be the unwitting heir to a noble French fortune, driven to crime by unrequited love and devoting most of his energies to aiding his rival and virtuous alter ego, Thames Darrell, and that Wild's evil machinations be prompted by unrequited love for Sheppard's mother, such matters are kept subordinate to 'accurate' if often extremely violent set-pieces depicting a criminal milieu red in tooth and claw. A highly ambivalent figure, Sheppard is on one level the Hogarthian 'idle apprentice', to be contrasted at every turn with the 'industrious' Thames, and prepared to rob his virtuous ex-employer Wood in a burglary which ends in the murder of Wood's wife; on another, he is – increasingly – the defender of all that is good and virtuous against the diabolical Wild's apparently unstoppable reign of terror, controlling simultaneously, as it does, both the world of crime and that of law-enforcement.

In form, the novel clearly owes a great deal to 'drama (melodrama we ought to say)', as Ainsworth puts it when summing up his earlier novel *Rookwood* (1834).[2] Despite many passages of painstakingly accurate description of routes through eighteenth-century London, the pith of *Jack Sheppard* consists of a series of 'scenes' packed with coincidences (character A is always encountering B just as they are embarking on the crucial stage of plan C), violent struggles, stagy asides, overheard soliloquies and cries of 'Confusion!' Central characters are bludgeoned or stabbed apparently to death on several occasions, only to return as if unscathed for the next encounter; less central characters are routinely disposed of with varying degrees of brutality; a general air of life-or-death crisis hangs over the whole book from its first scene (of baby-rescuing and apparent mass-slaughter) to its last (Blueskin Blake unhistorically shot dead while trying to cut Jack down from the gallows). The few scenes of comedy and character-establishment almost always lead straight into further crises, and there is hardly any conversation on subjects not directly and immediately related to the plot.

If on one level all this makes Ainsworth a somewhat primitive novelist, on another it makes him a pioneer of the contemporary thriller. Many of the same qualities can be found in James Ellroy's *American Tabloid* (1995), a 'factionalized' account of the build-up to the assassination of President Kennedy, whose mixture of real and invented characters and plot-lines is somewhat similar to Ainsworth's. Rather as every aspect of eighteenth-century London seems to be controlled by Wild, America up to 1963 is seen as controlled by such historically actual but fictitionally elaborated powers-behind-the-scenes as Sam Giancana's Mafia, J. Edgar Hoover's FBI, the CIA, Jimmy Hoffa's Teamsters union and the rival billionaires Howard Hughes and Joseph Kennedy. In a fantastically corrupt scenario, all these interests (with only the possible exception of the last) are seen as complicit in numerous murders, the abortive Bay of Pigs invasion of Cuba, and finally the Kennedy assassination itself. Working for all or most of them in turn, the three main protagonists – Pete Bondurant, Kemper Boyd and Ward Littell – are fictional but, we are led to believe, plausible missing links in the 'real' story.

As with Ainsworth, we shift from (presumably) accurate, well-researched indicators of the period and the various settings, to a rhythmically spaced series of short, extremely violent scenes, which set up a regular expectation of more of the same with few, if any, pauses for relaxation or consideration of other matters. While the plot is at one level highly intricate, at another it works fairly simply as a device for maintaining the stress-level throughout, and supplying enough potential new corpses to fill 400-odd pages. If there is a 'message', it is (not unlike Ainsworth's) to fuel our suspicion of those in power in the not-too-distant past and perhaps encourage us to transfer it to their present-day successors. If there is complexity, it lies mainly in our sympathies shifting slightly between the three protagonists, of whom the apparently slickest is finally outstripped, then cynically killed, by the initially most idealistic, while the apparently most brutally murderous emerges as the hero on points thanks to a late-developing love-interest. Somewhere within the calculated discords of these resolutions can be heard the 'there but for the grace of God go I' motif of the Newgate narratives.

Just as *American Tabloid* could easily be held up as a prime example of the violence and apparent amorality of fiction today, so the Newgate novels of Ainsworth and others were increasingly condemned for these same qualities. Such condemnations had also affected the careers of the more sophisticated novelists Edward Bulwer-Lytton and Charles Dickens, who had earlier created more fictionalized but contemporarily relevant pictures of the underworld in *Paul Clifford* (1830) and *Oliver Twist* (1837–8). Both, however, energetically denied any desire to glamorize crime, and claimed to point the way to reform through better education of potential young offenders.[3] Hence Lytton shows his hero as precisely corrupted by Newgate culture, avidly reading the exploits of Dick Turpin as a child before turning highwayman himself; and in *Oliver Twist*'s carefully graduated depictions of Sikes, Fagin, the Artful Dodger, Nancy and Oliver, Dickens managed to retain much of the Newgate appeal while hitching it to a reform platform of impeccable morality.

With the increasing disapprobation of the fictional presentation of working-class criminals, however, such novelists began to turn their attention to more psychological depictions of crime as a hidden guilt gnawing away behind the scenes of respectable middle-class society. As Lytton put it, 'From depicting in "Paul Clifford" the errors of society, it was almost the natural progress of reflexion to pass to those which swell to crime in the solitary human heart';[4] hence, in *Eugene Aram* (1832), the initial focus is firmly on the virtuous lifestyle and forthcoming marriage of the otherworldly scholar Aram who, it turns out, has managed for years to conceal all evidence of a murder committed in a fit of aberration in his youth. Though Aram's story was also a staple of *The Newgate Calendar*, it differs sharply from more blood-and-thunder Newgate narratives in suggesting the psychological pressures of Aram's double life as the main focus of interest. To this interest Lytton adds the devotion of the fiancée who eventually dies of a broken heart, and the more-in-sorrow-than-anger investigations of her cousin Walter Lester, whose ne'er-do-well father turns out to have been Aram's victim.

A somewhat similar theme of outward respectability masking secret guilt recurs thirty years later in some of the 'sensation novels' of the 1860s. In Mary Elizabeth Braddon's *Lady Audley's Secret* (1862), which she dedicated to Lytton, the murderous and bigamous Lucy Audley is presented as a figure of great power and fascination despite her increasingly desperate attempts to cover her traces. While she is treated with less of the somewhat subversive sympathy Lytton reserves for Aram, and though we are offered an easier alternative focus of identification in the hero Robert Audley who fills out the Walter Lester role, the novel has considerable shock-value in its demonstration of the subterfuges an apparently adoring Victorian wife may be driven to for survival. What is also striking is that the locus of hidden crime has become the here and now – unlike *Eugene Aram*, set safely in the eighteenth century, or the traditional gothic mode, whose exotic settings provided distance in space if not in time. What is also striking is the newly active role given to a woman, at least until she is finally declared insane in a solution which only partly removes the anxiety her independent spirit might arouse among Braddon's readers. To some extent because of such transgressions of gender stereotypes, the sensation novel soon followed the Newgate novel as a cause for moral concern and then repudiation.[5]

The two novels just discussed share with other novels such as Wilkie Collins's *The Woman in White* a bifurcation of interest between the doings of the guilty parties and protagonists who are, to a greater or lesser extent, detectives. In Walter Lester, Robert Audley and Collins's Marianne Halcombe and Walter Hartright, it could be argued that we have precursors of some of the amateur-detective protagonists discussed in the previous chapter. Indeed, as the ambivalent sympathies of the sensation novel receded under a cloud of suspicion, such characters had only to take a small further step towards centre-stage to produce the more straightforward struggle between goodies and baddies characteristic of the 'anti-conspiracy thriller' mode to be discussed in the following section, or of detective fiction itself.

In Britain, arguably, apart from some exceptions in 'high' literature, or in some of the semi-spoofs discussed in the previous chapter, the glamorous or sympathetic criminal now largely disappeared from popular fiction until well into the twentieth century. It was in the USA that such figures forcefully re-emerged as primary objects of reader identification, in what might be termed the *noir* thriller proper. Two factors may lie behind this: a long puritan-influenced literary tradition, focusing on individual souls predestined either to good or evil; and a still-current awareness – from the heroized Wild West to the 1920s Prohibition of alcohol – of criminality as at least an understandable career choice for ordinary people. Hence W. R. Burnett's *Little Caesar* (1929) offers a Newgate-like 'there-but-for-the-grace-of-God' account of the rise and fall of a Chicago gangster; while James M. Cain's *The Postman Always Rings Twice* (1934) and *Double Indemnity* (1936) are both laden with a sense of predestined damnation in their accounts of *folie-à-deux* adulterous couples impelled towards murder by their all-too-human lusts.

The deliberately deadpan tone of *Little Caesar* provides a very effective rhetoric for shocking the reader into accepting that there are people for whom gangland violence is a normal way of life. The only apparent moral commentary lies in the ironic disparity between the words and described feelings of the characters and the actual life-and-death situations they confront, as when the protagonist Rico contemplates the corpse of a former gang-partner he has killed: 'Somehow he had expected Tony to be changed. He was not. Here lay the same Tony who used to play poker with such fury. The same Tony, yes, only dead'.[6] Just before his own death, Rico addresses 'for the first time in his life a vague power which he felt to be stronger than himself', but only to implore 'Give me a break! Give me a break!' and then 'Mother of God, is this the end of Rico?'[7] – a question which receives its tacit answer in the blanking-out of the book at this point. Here, and as so often reworked since, the deadpan style hovers ambivalently between social indignation – 'This is what human beings can descend to if we fail to change this rotten society' – and a kind of existential admiration – 'These are the bare bones of the human condition, which only those who live on the edge can see in their true starkness'.

By contrast to the naturalist intentions and cold gaze of the gangster thriller (as in Lytton's turn from 'the errors of society...to those which swell to crime in the solitary human heart'), Cain's *Double Indemnity* explores the psychological motives and consequences of a crime of passion hatched after a chance meeting between two apparently 'normal' middle-class people. Written in the form of a confession by the insurance agent Walter Huff, it describes his rapid slide from discussing her husband's insurance with the *femme fatale* Phyllis Nirdlinger to plotting his murder in a way which will yield the 'double indemnity' bonus of the title. The equally rapid estrangement of the guilty pair after the murder, leading to the revelation that Phyllis has killed before and plans to do so again, hammers home the Faustian moral that crime contains its own nemesis, psychologically as well as legally. The legal nemesis is represented by the sleuthing activities of Phyllis's stepdaughter Lola (to whose now-unattainable innocence Huff is increasingly drawn) and Huff's insurance colleague Keyes, who (somewhat improbably) allows the doomed pair to escape the country on a liner in the knowledge that they have no choice but suicide. As the final moment arrives, the literary antecedents of the satanic *femme fatale* motif are loud and clear:

> She's in her stateroom getting ready. She's made her face chalk white, with black circles under her eyes and red on her lips and cheeks ... She looks like what came aboard the ship to shoot dice for souls in the Rhyme of the Ancient Mariner.
>
> I didn't hear the stateroom door open, but she's beside me now while I'm writing. I can feel her.
>
> The moon.[8]

The quasi-Faustian theme of a chance meeting between strangers which condemns one or both to perdition receives perhaps its best treatment in Patricia Highsmith's *Strangers on a Train* (1949). Eerily shifting the key from the sexual to something less easily definable (at least in the late 1940s), the novel describes a drunken proposition by one of the eponymous strangers, Charles Bruno, to kill the separated wife of the other, Guy Haines, if Guy will return the favour by killing Bruno's father: since there is no connection between the two beyond a single chance meeting, this will be the perfect crime. Though guiltily wishing his unfaithful wife out of the way so that he can marry again, the respectable if ambitious Guy is horrified first to learn of her murder, and then by Bruno's increasingly reckless reappearances in his life, which eventually impel him to play his part in the pact he never agreed to, and kill Bruno's father. As with all Faustian pacts, the freedom sought proves illusory, as

Bruno worms his way further and further into Guy's life before drunkenly drowning himself on a boating party, after which Guy sees no option but to give himself up. Such a bare outline of the plot (which Raymond Chandler saw as simply incredible when working on the screenplay for Hitchcock's film) does little to convey the novel's growing sense of claustrophobic inevitability, springing in part from the *doppelgänger*-like pairing of the outwardly capable and 'brilliant' architect Guy, and the childish, mother-fixated Bruno, who operates as a Dionysian id to Guy's Apollonian ego.

Many of Highsmith's other novels feature similar quasi-homoerotic bondings between men 'linked to each other by the idea of crime'.[9] In *The Talented Mr Ripley* (1957), a disturbed young man kills another whom he greatly admires, in order more or less to take over his identity, and then – in one of the great surprise endings of apparently genre-based fiction – gets away with it. This (decreasingly surprise) ending is reprised in three later novels written from 1970 to 1980, where Ripley commits several more unpunished murders. Whereas this sequence can be related to a growing amoralism in the thriller form generally, Highsmith also uses it to raise the question she poses in her *Plotting and Writing Suspense Fiction*: whether society really cares about the human cost of murder, or simply enjoys the vicarious sadism of identifying with the police.[10]

In Britain, the thriller aiming to take us inside a criminal's mind has also flourished, though rarely quite with Highsmith's sureness of impact. One early such work of the 'golden-age' era was *Malice Aforethought* (1931) by Francis Iles, an alternative name for the detective writer Anthony Berkeley. Following in blow-by-blow fashion the stages of an apparently inoffensive country doctor's meticulously planned murder of his wife, the novel carries an in-built safety net in the comedic style typical of much golden-age writing, and in its representation of the kind of case (for example, that of Dr Crippen) whose middle-class 'understandability' is celebrated with loving irony in George Orwell's essay 'The Decline of the English Murder' (1946). More recently, the criminal-centred thriller has been taken in more disturbing directions by Julian Symons (for instance, in *The Players and the Game*, based on the Moors Murders, 1972) and become one of the several provinces of Ruth Rendell, both under that name and as Barbara Vine. In one early Rendell novel, *A Judgement in Stone* (1977), a housemaid tormented by her own illiteracy turns her frustrations on her middle-class employers by killing them, with the help of an ally enlisted in the *folie à deux* tradition of Cain or Highsmith. While the bizarre motivation gives the novel some claim to be extending the thriller form towards a more weighty investigation of Britain's inarticulate obsession with class differences, the actual denotations of these differences are sometimes in danger of sinking the enterprise through oversignification.

In both Britain and America, the criminal-centred thriller has sometimes been twinned with the detective story to produce a split-level narrative in which we first witness the crime, then the investigation, and the suspense hinges on how the criminal will be caught rather than on his or her identity. An early example of this structure can be found in some of R. Austin Freeman's stories featuring Dr Thorndyke (particularly *The Singing Bone*, 1912), and a later one in the immensely popular American TV series of the 1960s, *Colombo*. Insofar as the emphasis here is on the final triumph of the detectives in uncovering the clues that actually prove their antagonists' guilt, this form can be seen as a branch of the whodunnit, in which the criminals generally remain psychologically blank except in their role as arrogantly clever coverers of their tracks. But with just a relatively small push in the direction of making the criminal's disturbingly self-justifying view of the world believable, and placing the main narrative interest in the cat-and-mouse duel between this view and that of the hero, the form has revived strongly since the 1980s – for example in the Elmore Leonard novels discussed in the last chapter – as one very effective development of the techniques and insights of the *noir* thriller.

[handwritten: minette Walters, The Dark Room]

4

The Anti-Conspiracy Thriller

[handwritten annotations: Sins threatened still by meg's brother - ameisa is also dangerous force - danger it she remembers]

To recapitulate: the thriller highlights danger within the present rather than (merely) the past action, hence its protagonists must be threatened by powerful forces of some kind. If these forces are seen as wicked and the protagonists as good, we are in the presence of an anti-conspiracy thriller.

Narratives in which heroes and heroines confront powerful adversaries are, of course, as old as fiction itself, from epics such as *The Odyssey* to fairy tales and Arthurian romances. Taking up the story in the late eighteenth century, the gothic novel repeatedly pits a heroine and, sometimes, her admirer against a patriarchal villain whose panoply of servants and imprisoning buildings betokens a power which is made to feel systemic rather than merely individual. Some of the radical implications of this structure are made more explicit in 'Jacobin novels' of the 1790s, such as Mary Wollstonecraft's unfinished *Maria, or The Wrongs of Woman* (1798), where the powers of patriarchy are symbolized in the madhouse to which the heroine is confined for attempting to escape from her miserable marriage. In the most influential such novel, William Godwin's *Caleb Williams* (1794), a somewhat similar attempt by the servant Caleb to escape from his employer Falkland, whom he has discovered to have committed a murder, leads to a powerful imagery whereby the whole of Britain becomes a 'Bastille', penetrated everywhere by the power of Falkland's gentry class and its spies and agents. Repeatedly imprisoned, dogged and defamed, Caleb finally brings his accusation to court, after which, in the published version, Falkland confesses and dies and the persecution ceases; though in an unpublished earlier version the claustrophobic

43

atmosphere is sustained till the end, as Caleb dies raving in the prison cell to which he is returned after the failure of his case.[1]

Because the early part of the book focuses closely on Caleb's gradual uncovering of his master's guilt – and perhaps also because Godwin's account of the novel's 'backwards' construction, from dénouement to starting point, interested and may have influenced Poe – some critics, such as Julian Symons, have seen *Caleb Williams* as a major precursor of the detective genre.[2] However, as Ian Ousby has pointed out, it works even more powerfully as a critique of the ethos of detection, in which Falkland's hired sleuth or 'spy', Gines, is easily the novel's most despicable character (not least for his desertion of the gang of thieves led by the idealistic Captain Raymond), and in which even Caleb's own detective work is presented as morally highly ambivalent.[3] At a time when government spies were interpenetrating Godwin's own radical circles, some of whose leading members came very close to being hanged on their evidence, it is hardly likely that he would support the ideology of policing as a guarantee of social stability on which the detective form implicitly depends. What *Caleb Williams* does strikingly anticipate, however, is the kind of anti-conspiracy thriller in which an isolated, possibly flawed but ultimately justified protagonist struggles against social or political forces too powerful to be overcome by a simple naming of their crimes.

It would be pointless to attempt an outline of all adventure stories and romances since the 1860s in which the good oppose the bad in some way; nonetheless, a distinct and recognizable subgenre which does deserve briefly tracing from later in the nineteenth century is that of spy fiction. Tales of political/ military intrigue, secret messages and crossing enemy lines incognito had long been familiar in the historical novels of Sir Walter Scott, James Fenimore Cooper and Alexandre Dumas;[4] as with comparable moves from the gothic and Newgate novels, it was in the updating of these motifs to a sharply contemporary setting that the modern spy genre came into being. In the work of William Le Queux (beginning with *Guilty Bonds*, 1890), Rudyard Kipling (*Kim*, 1901), Erskine Childers (*The Riddle of the Sands*, 1903), John Buchan (*The Thirty-Nine Steps*, 1915) and 'Sapper' (*Bulldog Drummond*, 1920), an enduring picture was built up of a British Secret Service actively and heroically dedicated to thwarting enemy agents and defending impressively modern-sounding military secrets. Clearly, the approach of the First World War helped to focus public attention on the theme, and on Germany as an enemy of appropriately terrifying power. In *The Thirty-Nine Steps*, the sense that the enemy is 'everywhere' provides an echo of *Caleb Williams* in the flight-and-pursuit motif whereby the hunted hero Richard Hannay is incapable of reporting his plight to the authorities because they, too, have been manipulated or at least misled by the ubiquitous enemy.[5]

After the Russian Revolution of 1917, Germany was soon superseded as chief public enemy by the Soviet Union, with its readily identifiable fifth column within the British labour movement. As early as 1920, *Bulldog Drummond* was using this additional ingredient to fuel right-wing beliefs that the war against foreigners (all routinely seen as despicable) was also the war against socialism at home. Hence *The Black Gang* (1922) opens with a secret meeting between a Russian agent (who strangely cries 'Mein Gott!' when alarmed), a disaffected businessman, three representatives of 'the poorer type of clerk...with that smattering of education which is the truly dangerous thing',[6] a professional burglar and two Jews. These last are later vaguely described as white slavers, but not before being flogged with relish 'to within an inch of their lives'[7] by Bulldog Drummond's Black Gang, whose masks and cloaks provide an interesting British link between the Ku Klux Klan and such caped and masked crusaders as Superman and Batman.

Drummond is, of course, a gentleman to his fingertips, liaising with his gang at their exclusive club and on nickname terms with the Chief of CID, for whom he fagged at school. Though married to the plucky Phyllis he is repeatedly targeted by the vampish Irma, the sidekick and presumably mistress of Drummond's chief antagonist, the villainous mastermind Carl Peterson. Apart from the marriage, this set-up closely anticipates that of many of Ian Fleming's James Bond novels (beginning with *Casino Royale*, 1953), where a counter-espionage role given general validity by the Soviet threat routinely focuses itself instead on the activities of a single mastermind, generally vaguely mid-European and assisted by a siren-like female accomplice with cold-hearted sexual designs on the hero.

If in the 'recovery time' after each of the two world wars, in the 1920s and early 1950s, there was a public taste for jingoistic self-assertion and a need for reassurance that any future threats could be nipped in the bud by extreme and prompt action, at other periods international tensions have become the focus of rather more thoughtful kinds of anxiety. In some of the novels of Graham Greene up to and concerning the Second World War, spying becomes an almost metaphysical test of loyalties and identities: in *The Ministry of Fear* (1943), for instance, the hero's unwitting entanglement with Nazi agents and his subsequent bomb-induced amnesia interact powerfully with a haunting sense of guilt about his wife's death and a wish to reinvent an identity from scratch. Treading in the footsteps of Greene and Eric Ambler (another writer of left-leaning spy-thrillers from the 1930s), John le Carré produced in such novels as *The Spy Who Came in from the Cold* (1963) a far more reflective view of the post-1945 Cold War stalemate than Fleming's novels of the 1950s or their many British and American counterparts.

We meet the hero, Alec Leamas, at a moment of disaster as the last of the ring of East German spies he runs is shot trying to cross from East to West Berlin: somehow the ruthless East German intelligence chief Mundt has learnt of Leamas's network and mopped it up. In a plan carefully set up by the head of British Intelligence, Leamas pretends to leave the service in disgrace and go on the skids, in the hope that Eastern Bloc agents will induce him to defect, whereupon he will apparently unwittingly give them evidence implicating Mundt as a double agent working for the West. This all happens as planned and, at a climactic secret trial in East Germany, Mundt is faced with this evidence by Leamas's debriefer, the sympathetic and intelligent Fiedler. In a demonic twist, however, Mundt produces a witness in the shape of Liz, Leamas's girlfriend from the period when he was apparently on the skids. Lured to the East through her naïve pro-communism, and unaware of what is going on, Liz unknowingly reveals that British agents carefully paid Leamas's debts after his 'defection', thus enabling Mundt to prove that Leamas has been sent to discredit him, and to order Fiedler's arrest as his accomplice. In a further twist, Liz and Leamas are secretly released at dead of night and driven to the Berlin Wall with instructions as to how and where they can cross it safely: clearly the whole story about Mundt working for the West was true, and Leamas and Liz have been pawns of Mundt and his British masters to discredit and remove the increasingly suspicious Fiedler. Portrayed as an unreconstructed Nazi with a special hatred of Jews such as Fiedler and Liz, and aware that as an idealistic non-spy Liz knows too much, Mundt (it is implied) orders her to be shot by the guards, who have turned a blind eye to Leamas's escape until it is Liz's turn to climb the wall after him. Facing a final existential choice between his natural feelings, represented by Liz, and the voice of the agent Smiley on the Western side exhorting him to jump for freedom, Leamas chooses the former: to truly come in from a cold in which both sides play equally foul, can only be to die.

Clearly, here, the black-and-white simplicities of Sapper or Fleming have given way to a far more self-doubting shade of grey, even though the ultimate rightness of the West's ideal of freedom, and wrongness of the communist sacrifice of means to ends, still structure the sense of repeated moral betrayal on which the shock of the novel's twists depends. And in the figure of the crypto-Nazi Mundt, relied on equally by the two ideologies once apparently defined by their hostility to Nazism, postwar confusions are still thrown into their clearest relief by reference back to the wartime moral certainties they have replaced.

In a series of increasingly lengthy later novels, le Carré explores similar ambivalences, if slightly less astringently thanks to the firm moral centre provided by his longstanding series-hero George Smiley (whose complicity in the Mundt plot despite an apparent fastidiousness about it is one of the best-prepared shocks of *The Spy Who Came in from the Cold*). While 'The Circus' of MI6 remains riddled with deceptions directed from the top, and political bad faith is still repeatedly mirrored in various gruesome emotional betrayals, the growing certainty of Smiley's long-term survival becomes increasingly identified with that of the rightness at the heart of the Western intelligence effort, even in what the title of an earlier (1965) novel memorably defined as a *Looking Glass War*.

With the ending of the Cold War in 1989 there was, not unnaturally, much speculation about the future of spy fiction. But just as the 'end of history' propounded by such visionaries as Francis Fukuyama (in *The End of History and The Last Man*, 1993) proved a mirage almost immediately, so did the 'end of spy fiction', at least as far as le Carré was concerned. Already in 1989, *The Russia House* depicted rather more accurately than most press reports the shock to the militantly dualistic Western mind-set administered by the discovery of the USSR's military impotence. Following in the footsteps of 1983's *The Little Drummer Girl*, dealing with the Arab–Israeli conflict in entirely non-Circus terms, le Carré has gone on to explore the fall-out from the Cold War's collapse in the shapes of international arms-dealing – *The Night Manager* (1993) – and revived small-state nationalism within the old Soviet empire – *Our Game* (1995), whose title deliberately invokes the 'great game' of Kipling's *Kim*, arguably the first and greatest British spy story, and similarly revolving round great-power ambitions in Central Asia.

Our Game's final discovery of new kinds of political commitment in the snowy mountains of a breakaway Russian republic also seems to reflect a wider current enthralment with the frozen wastes of the world: Peter Høeg's *Smilla's Sense of Snow* (1992, translated from Danish 1993) and Lionel Davidson's *Kolymsky Heights* (1994) both send their undercover protagonists to the Arctic Circle on rather similar missions to uncover ecological scandals hitherto sheltered behind the secrecies of the scientific establishment, big business or the Cold War status quo. All three novels include maps of areas of which most of their readers can be assumed to be completely ignorant: le Carré's Ingushetia, Høeg's Greenland and Davidson's Siberia and Bering Sea. There is here perhaps a renewal of the desire to introduce readers to the undiscovered places of the earth that inspired such bards of empire as Kipling and Conrad a century ago. But, with the southern Asia and Africa they wrote about now firmly the literary territory of the once-colonized rather than the colonizers, it is in the snowy wastes that the new imaginative territory is to be found: with, perhaps, a subliminal play on the imagery of a post-Cold-War 'unfreezing' of long-buried and potentially fatal secrets.

Rather than being spy stories proper, the three books just mentioned belong more to an adjacent type of anti-conspiracy thriller involving a single individual's lone struggle against some powerful political force, without the presumed back-up provided by the friendly state in spy fiction. One such novel, Geoffrey Household's *Rogue Male* (1939), describes the flight of the would-be assassin of a Hitler-like dictator from agents whose remorseless pursuit of him is constantly described in terms of the lore and language of hunting. Another game to the finish, dominated by similar hunting metaphors though with less sense of political endorsement, is the theme of *The Day of the Jackal* (1971) by Frederick Forsyth, who has spawned numerous imitators and gone on to make a fortune from similar outlines of quest and pursuit. In the cinema, the lone-hero action movie has too many examples to make any one really worth singling out: we are back to the problem that the anti-conspiracy subgenre easily expands to fit almost any kind of adventure from medieval romance onwards.

One other type of anti-conspiracy narrative worth mentioning, however, is what might be termed the amnesia thriller. By definition this subgenre hovers very close to, and sometimes belongs to, the *noir* thriller, since it concerns a protagonist whose loss of memory usually includes whether or not they themselves are guilty of a crime. Since it usually involves the protagonist finally piecing the truth together, it also often resembles or becomes a branch of the whodunnit. Hence one of its major early examples is Wilkie Collins's *The Moonstone*, whose hero Franklin's belated discovery that he himself stole the diamond while in an opium trance has already been discussed. As we shall see in the following chapter, the motif also fits in well with the less chiselled certainties of a private-eye detective thriller such as Dashiell Hammett's *Red Harvest*, whose hero spends the last quarter of the book trying to explain to himself strong evidence that he has killed the heroine while on a similar opium high. Other *noir*-ish American thrillers involving the theme include Cornell Woolrich's *The Black Curtain* (1941), John Franklin Bardin's *Devil Take the Blue-Tail Fly* (1948) and Stanley Ellin's *Mirror Mirror on the Wall* (1972) – all of which use the loss or repression of memory to explore disturbed states of mind and, often, to stretch the convention of the reliable narrator to near breaking point.[8] In Britain, Graham Greene's *The Ministry of Fear* (1943) fuses the convention with the spy story to great effect, making the hero's amnesia a blessed illusion of innocence against which he has to fight at a level affecting his whole sense of identity before he can re-engage with the political exigencies of the wartime present.

A recent work which fuses a great many of the elements described above in a brilliantly ludic way is Paul Verhoeven's film *Total Recall* (1990), starring Arnold Schwarzenegger. As in the post-Cold-War thriller, it involves ecological skullduggery by big business interests beyond the periphery of the known world, and, as in the amnesia thriller, its hero is ignorant not just of what he has done but who he is, and whose side he is really on. The film is set in the future; the further flung of its two settings is Mars, and the hero's shifts of memory are brought about by memory-implants which may mean that the entire action is illusory. All these facts bear testimony to the fluidity of the barriers supposedly separating one popular genre from another: science fiction, anti-conspiracy thriller, triple-cross spy story, *noir*ish redemption plot and metaphysical whodunnit are blended together in a concoction which finally makes perfect if wholly ambiguous sense. I shall return in the Conclusion to some implications of this interpermeability of genres I have devoted most of this study to trying to separate.

5

The Detective Thriller

The 'detective thriller' combines elements of all three of the forms described above. Its protagonist is most typically a private eye, who spends considerable time uncovering a past mystery but whose solitary, unofficial and employed status ensures that he or she is also involved in a struggle with powerful forces in the present tense of the narrative. These can include the police and, to the extent that the detective's need to protect the client's interests involves bending or breaking the law, the genre has some of the qualities of the *noir* thriller. Insofar as the detective is prone to direct threat from criminals, often professional and/or interlinked in ways which only gradually become clear, it also has characteristics of the anti-conspiracy thriller. At the same time, there is generally a whodunnit-like puzzle to be solved by the end, although here, given that straightforward murders are the province of the police, the detective often stumbles across them in the course of following up some more private matter for the client.

The existence of a client is one of the crucial factors differentiating the form. The fact that he or she has theoretically paid for the detective's loyalty can then often be used to signal the inequities of a system in which money can be thought to buy justice, in such set-piece situations as the detective's refusal to pocket the money or (even more commonly) the final revelation that the client or someone close to them is the real criminal. This often works to bring satisfyingly full-circle what began as a close-to-home private investigation into a blackmail message or a missing person, and only gradually spiralled outwards into the network of interrelated plots, leading the detective on an odyssey through ever-shifting milieux, which is another characteristic of the form.

Insofar as he is a 'consulting detective' available for hire, Sherlock Holmes sometimes anticipates later private-eye heroes in going well outside the law and in expressing moral contempt for (if not exactly refusing) the payments pressed on him by his wealthier clients. Both these features occur in the very first short story, 'A Scandal in Bohemia'. But the mixture of elements which characterize the private-eye detective thriller as a separate subgenre only came fully together in America in the 1920s, in the short stories published in the magazine *Black Mask*, edited by Joseph T. Shaw (1926–36).

The title is, perhaps, less indicative of the new set of conventions it nurtured than of the older ones they helped to replace: the mask of the highwayman, the raised neckerchief of the Wild West bankrobber, and the theatrical disguises of such otherwise urbane righters of wrongs as Zorro or Bulldog Drummond. By updating similar adventure and detective motifs to the harshly contemporary world of crime thrillers such as Burnet's *Little Caesar*, where such disguise has all but ceased to be necessary, and heeding Shaw's insistence on realism of character-portrayal as well as setting, the hardboiled private-eye story created something new. Though the most celebrated early examples of the genre are the novels of Dashiell Hammett and Raymond Chandler, both writers began their careers with *Black Mask*-style short stories, many of whose characters, detectives and even plots they transposed wholesale into their novels.

The first, and arguably still the most seminal, of these novels was Hammett's *Red Harvest* (1929), whose unnamed first-person hero, the Continental Op, had already featured in several *Black Mask* stories. Called in to investigate corruption in the mining town of Personville ('Poisonville' to its inhabitants) by Donald Willson, an idealistic newspaper editor who is then promptly murdered, the Op is instead hired to investigate the crime and then ultimately 'clean up' the town by the editor's father, the mine owner Elihu Willson. But Willson senior is obviously himself the major source of the town's problems, having in his efforts to break a miners' strike brought in the hoodlums who now run all the rackets. Though entirely void of sympathy for his client, the Op takes him at his word (and incidentally fulfils the oedipally subversive mission of his dead son, the discovery of whose killer constitutes only a minor 'first movement' of the plot): by apparently siding with the various gangs, one of which happens to be the city police force, and then double-crossing them all, he finally induces them to virtually wipe each other out in the cathartic 'harvest' after which the novel is named. Sexually involved with almost all the major players, including both Willsons and the Op himself, is the *femme fatale* Dinah Brand, whom the Op spends the last part of the book wondering whether he has himself murdered in an opium frenzy. The hero's self-doubt as to whether he has gone 'blood simple', the relatively sympathetic portrayal of Dinah and some of the leading hoodlums, and the sense that there is no way out of the situation created by his client but a bloodbath, are among the elements that lift the story from a straightforward contest of heroes and villains into something more challenging. In particular, as the 'red' of the title indicates, the story has a quite explicitly socialist message, that it is capitalism that has sown the wind of gangsterism, and will now have to reap the whirlwind.

Elements which this novel bequeaths to its many successors include the strong ambivalence towards the client, the routine police corruption, the *femme fatale*, the frequent sympathy and respect for at least some self-confessed criminals, and the strong identification of the detective with a missing or dead younger man whose sexual entanglements and conflicts with authority he himself seems to take on as the novel progresses. Whereas here this figure is the clearly dead Donald Willson (whose aim of cleaning up 'Poisonville' the Op takes on all too literally), in Raymond Chandler's *The Big Sleep* he is the more mysteriously missing Rusty Regan, the protégé of the detective Philip Marlowe's client General Sternwood. Initially hired by the General to investigate a blackmail threat against his daughter Carmen, Marlowe is repeatedly quizzed as to whether he was really hired to investigate Regan's disappearance – especially by Regan's wife, the General's other daughter Vivian. In the course of protecting Carmen from the consequences of her wild life as a drug-taking pornographic model at the centre of several murders, and incidentally fending off her advances, Marlowe seems to encounter Regan's trail at every turn, until finally the General does indeed hire him to follow it. Via a number of encounters with the ex-gangster Eddie Mars, a shoot-out with his vicious henchman Canino, and a growing intimacy with Vivian suddenly replaced by stronger feelings for Mars's wife Mona (with whom Regan also had an affair), Marlowe discovers that Regan is dead: he was shot by Carmen on refusing her advances under circumstances exactly replicated in Marlowe's own case, although Marlowe has made sure that this time she fires blanks. Vivian paid Mars to conceal the murder, and it was knowledge of this that ultimately lay behind the blackmail attempt Marlowe was first hired to investigate. Discreetly sharing his knowledge with the police, Marlowe keeps it from the General, while insisting that Vivian sends Carmen to a mental home.

It is an immensely complicated plot, in which the mystery involves not only who committed a specific crime, but what the real case to be solved actually is. Part of the sense of almost unnecessary complication results from the fact that the plots of two of Chandler's earlier short stories have been piled on top of each other, in a way designed to enhance the 'labyrinth' effect whereby a trail of apparently centrifugal leads ultimately only brings us back to the starting point.[2] Part also results from a dual focus whereby the detective thriller frequently oscillates between two types of story: one involving the seething domestic problems of a specific family (usually wealthy, often the client's), and one involving professional criminals representing the 'mean streets' down which the detective hero must go. The jump-cutting from one scenario to the other is what gives the form much of its tension, and the final binding of them together is a hallowed device for bringing out the corruption within outwardly respectable society, the stressing of which constitutes one of the form's main claims to be regarded as social criticism. Repeatedly, the formula runs that although the wider social corruption has not been cleared up it has at least been gestured at, while the problems of the family *are* solved in some suitably cathartic way.[3]

Arguably, it was the Prohibition of alcohol in the 1920s that really set up the conditions for the overlap between otherwise respectable citizens, suddenly criminalized for continuing to want a drink or two, and a new breed of ruthless gangster determined to supply it to them. But whereas this is precisely the theme of *Red Harvest*, by the time of *The Big Sleep* it has become a memory, treated almost with nostalgia in such touches as Rusty Regan's glamorous past as a bootlegger, the initial respect accorded to Eddie Mars who made his money the same way, and Marlowe's own atavistic rituals when drinking whiskey in a drugstore even though this is now perfectly legal elsewhere: '"My heart's in my mouth doing this," I said, and unscrewed the top of the whiskey bottle and loaded the coffee. "The law enforcement in this town is terrific"'.[4]

As this quote illustrates, the style Chandler gives to Marlowe as first-person narrator is often densely ironic, to the point where it is hard to tell the sound of a hard man spoofing the possibility that he might be scared (childish, effeminate, etc.) from that of a highly literate, educated writer subtly distancing himself from the 'hard' role he is meant to be playing. Indeed the solitary private eye's essentially vicarious relationship to the 'real' lives he discovers on his cases (reflected especially in his painstaking dogging of the sexual and other footsteps of a Donald Willson or Rusty Regan) can easily be read as evoking the writer's own vicarious participation in a realler, grittier world which he only fully encounters when 'on the case' of writing about it.

A writer who saw less need to distinguish between his own sensibilities and those of his hero was Ross Macdonald, who freely admitted that his protagonist Lew Archer was a projection of himself, and argued that Chandler's famously adulatory approach to Marlowe ('down these mean streets a man must go who is not himself mean') really expressed the profound sense of vulnerability that must underlie such a fantasy-projection.[5]

As might be guessed from this approach, Macdonald's work can be defined as the hardboiled plus psychoanalysis. In one of his more complex later novels, *The Underground Man* (1971), the theme of aberrant parenting as the source of most human woes is blazoned throughout, in the structuring of its dominant metaphors as well as of its plot. The 'missing man' whose trail Archer follows in time-honoured fashion is Stanley Broadhurst, to whose small son Ronny Archer becomes a surrogate father-figure at the start of the book. The discovery of Stanley's body in a shallow grave beneath which his own father is subsequently found buried indicates that the pressures which have damaged Stanley's relations with his son have to be tracked back to his own father's sins, from which most of the novel's many crimes ultimately spring. Another of the book's major metaphors, a forest fire designed to hide evidence of the two murders, seems to betoken the uncontrolled, snowballing destruction caused by attempts to repress past traumas into the unconscious or, as the title gestures, 'underground'. Apart from the boy Ronny, the other victim-figures Archer is most intent on saving are the adolescent Susan Crandall, who spends most of the book on the run from repressive parents intent on denying that she was raped as a child, and the retarded Fritz Snow. Fritz's oedipal bondage to his obsessively puritanical mother is only broken when she reveals herself, in a frenzied knife-attack on Archer, to be the madwoman behind much of the killing. If this climax recalls the revelation of female evil in Carmen Sternwood and other Chandler *femmes fatales*, it is significant that it is unequivocally as a repressive mother that Edna Snow fills out the familiar misogynistic pattern.

If there is a general social corruption in the novel equivalent to the criminal milieux of Hammett or Chandler, it is, more or less, that every family we encounter in outwardly prosperous California is riddled with parent–child breakdowns caused by the older generation's inability to tell the truth about its own failures. Since the plot is extremely complex, this involves far more characters than I have indicated, to the extent that such breakdowns are clearly indicated as systemic. Macdonald's shifting of the so-called 'hardboiled' form in increasingly liberal-reformist directions has been widely followed. While it is true that such writers as Mickey Spillane (flourishing in the 1950s) took it a long way in the opposite direction, towards anti-leftist paranoia and sadistic misogyny, many currently success-ful writers link it more or less explicitly to various reformist agendas. Recently, the most successful of these links has been with feminism.

The female private-eye novel began as an apparently paradox-ical contradiction in terms: from P. D. James's *An Unsuitable Job for a Woman* (1972) onwards, it has been used to challenge repressive gender stereotyping by putting a woman into a role usually thought of as archetypally masculine, and showing her succeeding against the odds. By the late 1990s, with the female private eye clearly a permanent feature of the landscape, it

gender

56

might be wondered how specifically 'male' the private eye ever really was. As a largely fantasy creation, an observant 'eye' on the contemporary scene who is also a relatively unencumbered first-person narrator easily identifiable with the private 'I' of the solitary reader, the traditional private eye is defined as male chiefly through two things: his social independence and his ability to withstand and sometimes use physical violence. The first of these is, however, part of what makes him a fantasy figure rather than an aspect of any irreducible social reality: whereas men tied to families and repetitive jobs can fantasize about a life of more authentic selfhood if free from such ties, women can use the role to imagine a much greater leap into full independence than the very partial moves in that direction which some have achieved in the last twenty or so years.

As for the familiarity with violence, this is a major topos of feminist private-eye fiction. Rather than being taken for granted as inevitable, it is most often something we see the heroine painfully and reluctantly pushed into. In James's *An Unsuitable Job*, after the suicide of her partner Bernie, the heroine Cordelia Gray inherits both his detective agency and his unlicensed gun, to which her attitude is at first not very serious: 'She had never seen it as a lethal weapon, perhaps because Bernie's boyishly naive obsession with it had reduced it to the impotence of a child's toy'.[6] As the plot thickens, she takes increasing care of it and eventually uses it to threaten a thug who has just tried to murder her, even though 'She knew that she wouldn't fire but, in that moment, she knew too what it was that could make a man kill'. Though 'She never knew whether he saw the gun', the thug kills himself in a car crash while fleeing from her, and when soon after this she is pestered by a lecherous drunk she has no hesitation in threatening him with it, though 'the menace in her voice struck cold even to her own ears'.[7] In her final confrontation with the main villain (who is also, with formulaic inevitability, the client) Cordelia surrenders the gun to his efficient secretary Miss Leeming, only to see her shoot him dead with it for what emerge as powerful reasons, whereupon Cordelia helps her to disguise the death as suicide by placing the victim's hands in the appropriate position, as Bernie had once taught her. In this shifting relationship with the gun, it is as if we also see Cordelia slowly familiarizing herself with the implications of the independence she has taken on: though she remains unable to pull the trigger herself, she has moved from seeing the gun as a boy's toy to seeing it as a necessary instrument of self-defence – while still wondering what 'could make a man kill' – and then to finding herself able actively to support another woman in using it.

Later feminist detective thrillers have dispensed with the last taboo on the heroine pulling the trigger. At the climax of Sue Grafton's first such novel *A is for Alibi* (1986), the heroine Kinsey Millhone's plight, on being hunted with a knife by her murderous ex-lover Charlie, is resolved with the simple four-word paragraph: 'I blew him away'.[8] Part of the kick delivered by these words comes from the implication that a whole fabric of male power and intimidation can be got rid of just as easily, with a breath as it were, once the right moment of resolution has been reached. That moment itself, however, is not reached easily: the book is avowedly written by Kinsey as a kind of therapy, and it begins and ends with the observations that 'The day before yesterday I killed someone and the fact weighs heavily on my mind', and 'The shooting disturbs me still. It has moved me into the same camp as soldiers and maniacs'.[9] The reference to soldiers points to the usual assumption of female private-eye narratives, that violence is institutionalized in male society in ways compared to which the heroine's occasional recourses to it will only ever be minimal.

When all this has been said, however, this closing sense of having become sullied by an alien set of values is not all that different from Marlowe's reflection at the end of *The Big Sleep*: 'Me, I was part of the nastiness now'.[10] In other respects too, the female private-eye story often simply reworks the conventions it might be thought to deconstruct, most notably perhaps in the straightforward substitution of the *femme fatale* by a figure who might be called the *homme fatal*, with whom the heroine has a sexual fling before discovering him to be deeply implicated in the murder she is investigating. In *A is for Alibi*, Charlie Scorsoni not only fulfils these requirements, but even surrounds himself with the same overblown whited-sepulchre decor as *The Big Sleep*'s vampish Vivian Regan. Compare 'The building itself looked like a Moorish castle: two stories of white adobe with windowsills two feet deep . . . The walls were white, hung with watercolours in various pastels' with 'The room was too big, the ceiling was too high, the doors were too tall, and the white carpet that went from wall to wall looked like a fresh fall of snow ... the enormous ivory drapes lay tumbled on the white carpet'.[11] Compare too the sexually appraising language of our first meetings with Charlie and Vivian: 'His collar was open, his tie askew, sleeves rolled up as far as his muscular forearms would permit. He was tilted back in his swivel chair with his feet propped up against the edge of the desk, and his smile was slow to form and smoldered with suppressed sexuality'; 'She was stretched out on a modernistic chaise-longue with her slippers off, so I stared at her legs in the sheerest silk stockings. They seemed to be arranged to stare at. They were visible to the knee and one of them well beyond ... she gave me a cool level stare over the rim of the glass'.[12]

The fact that female private eyes do sleep around (even if often in flings with *hommes fatals* they come to regret) is perhaps one of the gestures that began as a slap in the face to the traditional genre ('what would you think if a woman acted like that?') but with time has become a more straightforward assertion of the right to a non-monogamous lifestyle now available to both sexes. In one prevalent variant, the lesbian private-eye story (Barbara Wilson, Mary Wings, Katherine V. Forrest, and others), such sexual activity is essential to the polemical point being made, even while the sleeping-with-the-murderer convention returns us to the familiar figure of the *femme fatale* in another guise.[13]

If, as argued above, the social and occupational independence of the private eye forms an effective fantasy-focus for readers (and writers) of both sexes, the cult of solitude as an absolute good in itself is sometimes challenged by feminist writers of the genre. Writers such as Sara Paretsky, Gillian Slovo and Sarah Dunant provide their sleuths with ample networks of friends, relatives, and sometimes even male partners, who offer emotional support while being firmly debarred from much participation in the cases. While Hammett's, Chandler's and Macdonald's heroes also have a certain amount of back-up (and Hammett's *The Thin Man* even has a husband-and-wife team in Nick and Nora Charles), the image they offer is pre-eminently one of an emotional solitude that actually is, perhaps, more male than female. Or else, arguably, it is a solitude only claimable by the kind of individual accepted as the 'universal subject' of a given culture: in this case not only the male but the white middle-class male who really needs no further context to establish his identity.

In the detective thrillers of the African-American writer Walter Mosley, context is a crucial part of the point. Their hero, Easy Rawlins, exemplifies some of the difficulties of survival as a black in the overtly racist Los Angeles of the 1950s and early 1960s. Repeatedly pressured by the police or members of the white establishment to 'go into the places where they could never go...when the cops needed the word in the ghetto', Easy's effectiveness as a detective lies precisely in his rootedness in that society.[14] He is married, with a daughter and adopted son, runs a somewhat shady property company, and has a strong alter-ego-like friendship with a psychotic killer, Mouse, who often becomes a suspect in his cases but who also embodies Easy's own more violent impulses, restrained only with the greatest difficulty. If Mosley's novels keep in place and indeed intensify many conventions of the formula – the hostility to the police and distrust of the wealthy client, the personal danger, lonely footslogging and brief sexual encounters – it is in a context where such experiences are convincingly represented as the typical lot of any black male of the period attempting a kind of self-empowerment bound to position him uneasily between his own community and the white society where all the power resides.

In its various transmutations to accommodate the aspirations of disempowered groups, the hardboiled private-eye form has shown greater flexibility than might have been imagined from the many formulaic aspects that have often made it easy to parody. In fact this very susceptibility to parody has from the start been a part of the form itself: we have already looked at Philip Marlowe's intricate gavotte round the question of whether it is tough to drink whiskey in a drugstore, and another example might be Hammett's similar twirl around whether the renaming of Personville as Poisonville is a clever *mot juste* or just the result of a tough convict's accent: 'He also called his shirt a shoit'.[15] With its two leading practitioners so ready to position themselves somewhat askew of the hardboiled mannerisms they are busy inventing, it is not surprising that others have joined in the game, whether from the politically deconstructive viewpoints discussed above or from that of a more ludically deconstructive literary postmodernism – one or two examples of which I shall conclude this book by considering.

Conclusion

Throughout this book so far, I have tried to stick to the formal separation of crime fiction genres outlined in the Introduction. In fact, however, many interesting works and developments have sprung from the transgression or at least pushing-back of such generic boundaries, either out of dissatisfaction with their current limits or out of a more ludic urge to make the reader aware of their artificiality as cultural constructions.

The first type of development includes the more or less continuous attempt to make the whodunnit realistic or, if that is impossible, at least more apparently realistic than its previous metamorphoses. From Sherlock Holmes's sneers at Dupin's 'showiness' and Lecoq's 'slowness' onwards, whodunnit detectives have repeatedly adduced their fictional predecessors as the negative poles of before-and-after oppositions in which scientific modernity always favours the latter.[1] Hence, for Raymond Chandler, what I have called the detective thriller is chiefly defined in opposition to the kind of obsession with evidential detail and special knowledge which had once made the classic whodunnit seem so modern: 'Hammett gave murder back to the kind of people that commit it for reasons, not just to provide a corpse, and with the means to hand, not with hand-wrought duelling pistols, curare, and tropical fish'.[2] Since then, the rise of the police procedural (itself a return to the Lecoq-like 'slowness' pronounced so outmoded by Holmes) implicitly leapfrogs over the improbabilities of the private-eye mode towards the receding grail of reality, only to be trumped in turn by the array of continually updated technological computer wizardry and 'profiling' techniques summoned by Patricia Cornwell's forensic and psychological specialists.

The crimes, too, undergo periodic overhauls: the many

robberies Holmes investigates giving way in turn to the mandatory (usually single) murder of Christie, the more frequent 'murder for reasons' of the hardboiled, and the ubiquitous serial killer of today. Like the child sexual abuse which now features somewhere in the crime's background in numerous whodunnit and thriller plots (from Ross Macdonald to Andrew Vachss, who has put this crime at the centre of his vengeful, Spillane-like thrillers),[3] the serial-killer motif betokens realism partly because of a strong public fear of such things being on the rise, but also because of the way they seem to test the reader's ability to 'take' such shocking doses of reality on board. The sense of being educated to face and cope with worse things than one thought possible has arguably been one of the ambivalent pleasures of the form from the beginning. What must be expected, however, is that even serial killers and child abuse will eventually succumb to the charge of insufficient realism, precisely as they become seemingly ever more mandatory and built-in as requirements of the whodunnit formula itself.

A similar continual trumping of predecessors also obtains in the thriller. Within the anti-conspiracy thriller, the fairly black-and-white hero–villain struggles of Bulldog Drummond or James Bond (despite, again, much continuous 'scientific' updating) seemed for a time to be replaced by the murkier grey interzone of a writer such as le Carré, who uses whodunnit techniques to multiply plot-twists each of which uncovers a further betrayal of the good that was supposedly being defended. If the action-adventure genre has proved too robust for such replacement of its simplicities ever to be complete, a massive hit like the film *Total Recall* demonstrates how well the form has managed to absorb such motifs of betrayal and counter-betrayal into its apparently musclebound stride.

As for the *noir* thriller, many of its manifestations can be seen as themselves attempts to trump the detective whodunnit in the name of greater realism about criminals than can possibly be gathered from stories where their very identity is a mystery until the final pages. As well as denoting suspense, the eponymous 'thrill' here may also imply the excitement of drawing closer to the forbidden than one hitherto thought possible, certainly within the elaborate rules of concealment out of which the whodunnit is constructed. As already suggested, it is from the combination of these two opposed approaches that the 'murder for reasons' of the detective thriller emerges, even though this form generally remains scrupulous in its concealment of at least one major secret until the end. So powerful has *noir*'s implicit rhetoric of realism become in recent years, however, that in the 'split-level' narrative where detection is intercut with the criminal's own thoughts and actions (for example, Thomas Harris's *The Silence of the Lambs*), the whodunnit sometimes seems on the verge of conceding defeat prematurely, allowing the reader the pleasure of piecing clues together only up to the point where it seems more exciting to switch to direct hero–villain confrontation. Looked at from the other direction, this form also sacrifices one of the key challenges of the *noir* thriller proper, where our often painful recognition of the criminal's humanity cannot finally be ducked by any wholesale transfer of our sympathies to more law-abiding figures: a transfer which the split-level story seems specifically designed to perform.

The above are all transformations of what I have presented as the four basic genres of crime fiction, either in acknow-ledgement of pressures from one of the other three, or in the name of a (possibly ever-receding) goal of 'realism', or both. There are other transformations, however, where the crossovers are with types of writing not normally associated with crime fiction, and where realism is by no means the point. Indeed, here it is often the very artificiality and formulaic character of the crime genres that is emphasized, sometimes for the opportunities of game-playing offered by their apparently rigid sets of rules, and sometimes with the intention of bringing out the similarly 'constructed' and artificial nature of all literary narrative.

Plentiful examples of such game-playing are to be found within the genre itself, from G. K. Chesterton's self-conscious borrowing of whodunnit conventions to arrest us with novel arguments about politics, religion or aesthetics, to the detective Gideon Fell's notorious statement in John Dickson Carr's *The Hollow Men* that 'we're in a detective story, and we don't fool the reader by pretending we're not. Let's not invent elaborate excuses to drag in a discussion of detective stories. Let's candidly glory in the noblest pursuits [sic] possible to characters in a book'.[4] Elsewhere, postmodernist writers such as Alain Robbe-Grillet and Jorge-Luis Borges have made use of whodunnit and detective thriller techniques in a sort of mock-heroic formula, wherein a literary tradition is juxtaposed to a contemporary experience too complex for it, in ways which are not necessarily to the literary tradition's disadvantage. In Pope's *The Rape of the Lock* or *The Dunciad*, where the Homeric formulas are deliberately mismatched to their new subject matter, the mockery hovers between the heroic expectation and the unheroic reality which that expectation exposes. Similarly, it is an open question whether the coming-apart of the apparent 'case' in Robbe-Grillet's *Les Gommes* or Borges's 'The Garden of Forking Paths' or 'Death and the Compass' or *Six Problems for Don Isidro Parodi*[5] is a critique of the oversimplified solutions crime fiction has led us to expect, or a demonstration that the epistemological uncertainties of modern experience are best approached through formulas that do at least expect us to view life chiefly as a mystery.

One fairly recent example of what is by now quite a long tradition of postmodernist mock-detection is Paul Auster's *The New York Trilogy* (1988) which, in particular, explores the links between the 'lonely hero' of the private-eye detective thriller and the role of the writer. In the first of its three novellas, *City of Glass* (1985), the hero is a detective-thriller writer who 'like most people...knew almost nothing about crime'.[6] Nonetheless, mistaken for a detective called Paul Auster, he is hired to follow a man whose attempts to uncover profound truths by wandering apparently aimlessly round New York he eventually takes over on his own account. When he loses his quarry he simply continues his lonely vigil before mysteriously disappearing, leaving behind him only a red notebook concluding with the words 'What will happen when there are no more pages in the red notebook?'[7] On one level, the story suggests that there is no point in looking for ultimate meanings in essentially random experience, as the detective genre proposes; on another, it is a celebration of the kind of determination to find them nonetheless which characterizes both the obsessed private eye and the author, who similarly has no existence for the reader outside the necessary but doomed attempt to construct narrative meaning until 'there are no more pages'.

Since the pages of the present book are also running out, it will be useful to draw to a close with a quote from the start of *City of Glass*, where Auster explains the appeal of the detective story to the postmodernist writer certain that there are no irreducible 'essences' to be found, only a sharpened awareness of the equally significant 'existence' of discrete objects:

> Since everything seen or said, even the slightest, most trivial thing, can bear a connection to the outcome of the story, nothing must be overlooked. Everything becomes essence; the centre of the book shifts with each event that propels it forward ... In effect, the writer and the detective are interchangeable. The reader sees the world through the detective's eye, experiencing its proliferation of details as if for the first time. He has become awake to the things around him, as if, because of the attentiveness he now brings to them, they might begin to carry a meaning other than the simple fact of their existence.[8]

Or, as G. K. Chesterton put it in 1902,

> The lights of the city begin to glow like innumerable goblin eyes, since they are the guardians of some secret, however crude, which the writer knows and the reader does not. Every twist of the road is like a finger pointing to it; every fantastic skyline of chimney-pots seems wildly and derisively signalling the meaning of the mystery ... Anything which tends, even under the fantastic form of the minutiae of Sherlock Holmes, to assert this romance of detail in civilization, to assert this unfathomably human character in flints and tiles, is a good thing.[9]

Notes

CHAPTER 1. THE DETECTIVE WHODUNNIT FROM POE TO WORLD WAR I

1. Tsvetan Todorov, 'The Typology of Detective Fiction', in *The Poetics of Prose*, trans. R. Howard (Oxford: Basil Blackwell, 1977), 42–9.
2. W. H. Auden, 'The Guilty Vicarage', in *The Dyer's Hand and Other Essays* (London: Faber & Faber, 1948), reprinted in Robin W. Winks (ed.), *Detective Fiction: A Collection of Critical Essays* (Englewood Cliffs, NJ: Prentice-Hall, 1980), 15–24; see 15.
3. Edgar Allan Poe, 'The Philosophy of Composition', in *The Fall of the House of Usher and Other Writings* (London: Penguin, 1986), 480–92; see 482.
4. Poe, 'The Philosophy of Composition, *The Fall of the House of Usher*, 480–81.
5. See Ian Ousby, *Bloodhounds of Heaven: The Detective in English Fiction from Godwin to Doyle* (Cambridge, Mass.: Harvard University Press, 1976), Part I, especially 44–6; Dennis Porter, *The Pursuit of Crime: Art and Ideology in Detective Fiction* (New Haven: Yale University Press), 152 (on the New York Day and Night Police); Charles Dickens, 'The Detective Police', 'Three "Detective" Anecdotes', 'On Duty with Inspector Field' and 'Down with the Tide', in *The Uncommercial Traveller and Reprinted Pieces* (London: 1958); Edgar Allan Poe, 'The Murders in the Rue Morgue', in *The Fall of the House of Usher and Other Writings* (Harmondsworth, Middx.: Penguin, 1986), 204.
6. See especially Pierre Boileau and Thomas Narcejac, *Le Roman policier* (Paris: Vendôme, 1975), 37: 'melodrama [such as Gaboriau's] is precisely the foreign body that the detective novel needed to reject.'
7. Arthur Conan Doyle, *Memories and Adventures* (London: Hodder & Stoughton, 1924), 95.
8. Arthur Conan Doyle, *A Study in Scarlet* (1887), see *The Penguin Complete Adventures of Sherlock Holmes* (London: Penguin, 1981), 24–5.

9. e.g. *A Study in Scarlet*, 'The Five Orange Pips', 'The Adventure of the Red Circle', *The Valley of Fear*.

10. e.g. *The Sign of Four*, 'The Boscombe Valley Mystery', 'The Adventure of Black Peter'.

11. e.g. 'The Adventure of the Noble Bachelor', 'The Yellow Face', 'The Crooked Man'.

12. e.g. *The Hound of the Baskervilles*, 'The Adventure of the Speckled Band', 'The Adventure of the Copper Beeches'.

13. e.g. 'The Musgrave Ritual', 'Silver Blaze'.

14. e.g. 'A Scandal in Bohemia', 'The Adventure of the Beryl Coronet', 'The Adventure of the Priory School'.

15. e.g. 'A Case of Identity', 'The Man with the Twisted Lip'.

16. e.g. 'A Scandal in Bohemia', 'The Adventure of the Copper Beeches', 'The Yellow Face'.

17. e.g. 'The Adventure of the Beryl Coronet', 'The Adventure of the Engineer's Thumb'.

18. Arthur Morrison, 'The Affair of the "Avalanche Bicycle and Tyre Co., Limited"', from *The Dorrington Deed-Box* (1897), reprinted in Hugh C. Greene (ed.), *The Rivals of Sherlock Holmes* (Harmondsworth, Middx.: Penguin, 1971), 117.

19. G. K. Chesterton, 'A Defence of Detective Stories' (1902), reprinted in Howard Haycraft (ed.), *The Art of the Mystery Story* (New York: Carroll & Graf, 1983), 3–6.

CHAPTER 2. THE DETECTIVE WHODUNNIT FROM CHRISTIE TO THE PRESENT

1. See W. H. Auden, 'The Guilty Vicarage', in R. W. Winks, (ed.), *Detective Fiction*, 20.

2. For a useful reframing of this issue, see Alison Light, 'Agatha Christie and Conservative Modernity', in *Forever England: Femininity, Literature and Conservatism Between the Wars* (London: Routledge, 1991), chapter 2.

3. See Michelle B. Slung (ed.), *Crime on her Mind: Fifteen Stories and Female Sleuths from the Victorian Era to the Forties* (Harmondsworth, Middx.: Penguin, 1977).

4. Agatha Christie, *A Murder Is Announced* (London: HarperCollins, 1993), 50.

5. Ogden Nash, quoted in Julian Symons, *Bloody Murder: From the Detective Story to the Crime Novel: A History* (Harmondsworth, Middx.: Penguin, 1985), 103.

6. P. D. James, *Shroud for a Nightingale* (1973), in *A Dalgleish Trilogy*

(Harmondsworth, Middx.: Penguin, 1991), 49; *Original Sin* (Harmondsworth, Middx.; Penguin, 1996), 222: 'The room had obviously once been a dining-room but its elegance had been desecrated by the end partition which cut across the oval stucco decorations on the ceiling and bisected one of the four tall windows which looked out on Innocent Passage.'

CHAPTER 3. THE *NOIR* THRILLER

1. See Daniel Defoe, 'The True and Genuine Account of the Life and Actions of the Late Jonathan Wild' (1725) and 'The History of the Remarkable Life of Jack Sheppard (1724), in *The Selected Poetry and Prose of Daniel Defoe*, ed. Michael Shugrue (New York: Reinhardt Editions, 1968), 231–308; George Theodore Wilkinson, *The Newgate Calendar*, ed. C. Hibbert (London: Cardinal, 1991), 119–69.
2. William Harrison Ainsworth, *Rookwood* (London: J. M. Dent & Sons, 1931), 393.
3. Particularly in their Prefaces: see Lord Lytton (Edward Bulwer-Lytton), *Paul Clifford* (London: George Routledge & Sons, 1874), pp. vii–viii; and Charles Dickens, *Oliver Twist* (Harmondsworth, Middx.: Penguin, 1985), 34–5.
4. See 1848 Preface to edition of *Paul Clifford* cited above, p. xii.
5. See Kimberley Reynolds and Nicola Humble, *Victorian Heroines: Representations of Femininity in Nineteenth-Century Literature and Art* (New York and London: Harvester Wheatsheaf, 1993), 100–105; Lynn Pykett, *The Sensation Novel: from 'The Woman in White' to 'The Moonstone'* (Plymouth: Northcote House, 1994), 1–7.
6. W. R. Burnett, *Little Caesar* (London: Jonathan Cape, 1932), 88.
7. W. R. Burnett, *Little Caesar*, 252.
8. James, M. Cain, *Double Indemnity* (London: Pan, 1983), 120.
9. Julian Symons, *Bloody Murder: From the Detective Story to the Crime Novel: A History* (Harmondsworth, Middx.: 1985), 166.
10. Patricia Highsmith, *Plotting and Writing Suspense Fiction* (London: Poplar Press, 1983), 56.

CHAPTER 4. THE ANTI-CONSPIRACY THRILLER

1. See William Godwin, *Caleb Williams*, ed. D. McCracken (Oxford: Oxford University Press, 1982), 181, 319–34.
2. See Edgar Allan Poe, 'The Philosophy of Composition', *The Fall of the House of Usher*, 480; and Julian Symons, *Bloody Murder*, 28–31.
3. See Ian Ousby, *Bloodhounds of Heaven*, 20–42.

4. e.g. Sir Walter Scott, *Waverley* (1814), James Fenimore Cooper, *The Last of the Mohicans*, Alexandre Dumas, *Les Trois Mousquetaires* (1844).
5. The image of this chase is now perhaps more familiar from Alfred Hitchcock's 1935 film.
6. 'Sapper' (H. C. McNeile), *The Black Gang* (London: Hodder and Stoughton, 1922), 11.
7. 'Sapper', *The Black Gang*, 19.
8. Minette Walters's *The Dark Room* (Basingstoke: Macmillan, 1995) is an excellent recent British example of this subgenre.

CHAPTER 5. THE DETECTIVE THRILLER

1. See Stephen Knight, *Form and Ideology in Crime Fiction* (London: Macmillan, 1980), chapter 5.
2. The short stories are 'Killer in the Rain' and 'The Curtain', published in Raymond Chandler, *Killer in the Rain* (Harmondsworth, Middx.: Penguin, 1966).
3. See Stephen Knight, '"A Hard Cheerfulness": An Introduction to Raymond Chandler', in Brian Docherty (ed.), *American Crime Fiction: Studies in the Genre* (Basingstoke: Macmillan, 1988), 82–5.
4. Raymond Chandler, *The Big Sleep* (Harmondsworth, Middx: Penguin, 1948), 103.
5. Raymond Chandler, 'The Simple Art of Murder' (1944), in Howard Haycraft (ed.), *The Art of the Mystery Story: A Collection of Critical Essays* (New York: Carroll & Graf, 1983), 237; Ross Macdonald, 'The Writer as Detective Hero' (1973), in Winks (ed.), *Detective Fiction*, 182–5.
6. P. D. James, *An Unsuitable Job for a Woman* (London: Sphere, 1974), 14.
7. *An Unsuitable Job for a Woman*, 154, 156.
8. Sue Grafton, *A is for Alibi* (London: Pan, 1990), 253.
9. *A is for Alibi*, 7, 253.
10. *The Big Sleep*, 189.
11. *A is for Alibi*, 30; *The Big Sleep*, 16.
12. *A is for Alibi*, 32; *The Big Sleep*, 16.
13. e.g. Barbara Wilson, *Murder in the Collective* (London: Women's Press, 1984); Mary Wings, *She Came too Late* (London: Women's Press, 1986); Katherine V. Forrest, *The Beverley Malibu* (London: Pandora, 1989).
14. Walter Mosley, *White Butterfly* (London: Pan, 1994), 10. Not all of this applies to the first Rawlins novel, *Devil in a Blue Dress* (1990), set in 1948.

15. Dashiell Hammett, *Red Harvest*, (London: Pan, 1975), 5.

CONCLUSION

1. Sir Arthur Conan Doyle, *A Study in Scarlet* (1887), in *The Penguin Complete Adventures of Sherlock Holmes* (London: Penguin, 1981), 24–5.
2. Raymond Chandler, 'The Simple Art of Murder', in Howard Haycraft (ed.), *The Art of the Mystery Story*, 234.
3. e.g. Andrew Vachss, *Strega* (London: Pan, 1988).
4. John Dickson Carr, *The Hollow Man* (Harmondsworth, Middx.: Penguin, 1951), 186–7.
5. Alain Robbe-Grillet, *Les Gommes* (1953), translated as *The Erasers* (London: Calder & Boyars, 1965); Jorge Luis Borges, 'The Garden of Forking Paths' and 'Death and the Compass', both in *Labyrinths* (Harmondsworth, Middx: 1981); Jorge Luis Borges and Adolfo Bioy-Casares, *Six Problems for Don Isidro Parodi*, translated by N. T. di Giovanni (New York: E. P. Dutton, 1981).
6. Paul Auster, *The New York Trilogy* (London: Faber & Faber, 1987), 7.
7. *The New York Trilogy*, 131.
8. *The New York Trilogy*, 8.
9. G. K. Chesteron, 'A Defence of Detective Stories' (1902), in Howard Haycraft (ed.), *The Art of the Mystery Story*, 4–5.

Select Bibliography

FICTION

The editions are those from which I have quoted.

Ainsworth, William Harrison, *Rookwood* (London: J. M. Dent & Sons, 1931).

Auster, Paul, *The New York Trilogy* (London: Faber & Faber, 1987).

Bulwer-Lytton, Edward, *Paul Clifford* (London: George Routledge & Sons, 1874).

Burnett, W. R., *Little Caesar* (London: Jonathan Cape, 1932).

Cain, James, M., *Double Indemnity* (London: Pan, 1983).

Carr, John Dickson, *The Hollow Man* (Harmondsworth, Middx.: Penguin, 1951).

Chandler, Raymond, *The Big Sleep* (Harmondsworth, Middx.: Penguin, 1948).

Christie, Agatha, *A Murder is Announced* (London: HarperCollins, 1993).

Dickens, Charles, *Oliver Twist* (Harmondsworth, Middx.: Penguin, 1985).

Doyle, Sir Arthur Conan, *The Penguin Complete Adventures of Sherlock Holmes* (London: Penguin, 1981).

Godwin, William, *Caleb Williams* (Oxford: Oxford University Press, 1982).

Grafton, Sue, *A is for Alibi* (London: Pan, 1990).

Hammett, Dashiell, *Red Harvest* (London: Pan, 1975).

James, P. D., *Shroud for a Nightingale*, in *A Dalgleish Trilogy* (Harmondsworth, Middx.: Penguin, 1991).

———— *Original Sin* (Harmondsworth, Middx.: Penguin, 1996).

———— *An Unsuitable Job for a Woman* (London: Sphere, 1974).

Morrison, Arthur, 'The Affair of the "Avalanche Bicycle and Tyre Co., Limited"', in Hugh C. Greene (ed.), *The Rivals of Sherlock Holmes* (Harmondsworth, Middx.: Penguin, 1971).

Mosley, Walter, *White Butterfly* (London: Pan, 1994).

Poe, Edgar Allan, *The Fall of the House of Usher and other Writings*

(Harmondsworth, Middx.: Penguin, 1986).

'Sapper' (H. C. McNeile), *The Black Gang* (London: Hodder & Stoughton, 1922).

CRITICAL STUDIES

Auden, W. H., 'The Guilty Vicarage', in *The Dyer's Hand and Other Essays* (London: Faber & Faber, 1948), reprinted in Robin W. Winks (ed.), *Detective Fiction: A Collection of Critical Essays* (Englewood Cliffs, NJ: Prentice Hall, 1980). A brief, brilliant defence of the traditional whodunnit against the claims of 'art' and the hardboiled.

Bell, Ian A., and Graham Daldry (eds), *Watching the Detectives: Essays on Crime Fiction* (London: Macmillan, 1990). A useful collection of critical essays.

Bennett, Tony (ed.), *Popular Fiction: Technology, Ideology, Production, Reading* (London: Routledge, 1990). Contains an excellent selection of some recent theoretical work, in Sections 2, 4 and 6.

Bloom, Clive (ed.), *Twentieth Century Suspense* (Basingstoke and London: Macmillan, 1988). Like others in the Macmillan Insights series, a useful collection of critical essays.

———— *et al.* (eds), *Nineteenth-Century Suspense: From Poe to Doyle* (Basingstoke and London: Macmillan, 1988). See above comment.

Cawelti, John G., *Adventure, Mystery and Romance: Formula Stories as Art and Popular Culture* (Chicago: Chicago University Press, 1976). A densely packed, groundbreaking study of popular genres, in which 'crime fiction' is more prominent than the title suggests.

Dibdin, Michael (ed.), *The Picador Book of Crime Writing* (London: Picador, 1994). An intelligent choice of extracts indicating that the genre involves style as well as plots, with a particularly useful if brief selection of critical views in Part 3.

Docherty, Brian (ed.), *American Crime Fiction: Studies in the Genre* (Basingstoke and London: Macmillan, 1988). See comment on Clive Bloom above.

Eco, Umberto, *The Role of the Reader* (London: Hutchinson, 1979). A founding text in the application of semiotics to popular fiction, including a fascinating account of the structure of the series mode in chapters 4 – 6.

Haycraft, Howard (ed.), *The Art of the Mystery Story: A Collection of Critical Essays* (New York: Carroll & Graf, 1983). Contains many classic surveys of the subject, for example by G. K. Chesterton, Ronald Knox, Nicholas Blake and Raymond Chandler.

Highsmith, Patricia, *Plotting and Writing Suspense Fiction* (London: Poplar Press, 1983). More a 'how to' guide for aspirant suspense writers than a sustained work of theory or criticism, but still a quirky, often insightful exploration of the genre by its supreme exponent.

Knight, Stephen, *Form and Ideology in Crime Fiction* (London: Macmillan, 1980). One of the best books on the subject: centred on individual writers, but situates each clearly in a different historical moment.

Light, Alison, *Forever England: Femininity, Literature and Conservatism Between the Wars* (London: Routledge, 1991). Contains an important reassessment of Agatha Christie as a modernist writer, in chapter 2 (of four).

Mandel, Ernest, *Delightful Murder: A Social History of the Crime Story* (London: Pluto Press, 1984). A classic Marxist account of the hidden fears underlying the genre's popularity.

Most, Glenn W., and William W. Stowe (eds), *The Poetics of Murder: Detective Fiction and Literary Theory* (San Diego, New York and London: Harcourt Brace Jovanovich, 1983). Sadly out of print, but still the best collection of essays on the genre from the angle of literary theory.

Munt, Sally, *Murder by the Book? Feminism and the Crime Novel* (London: Routledge, 1994). A thoughtful application of recent feminist theory to crime writing.

Ousby, Ian, *Bloodhounds of Heaven: The Detective in English Fiction from Godwin to Doyle* (Cambridge: Mass.: Harvard University Press, 1976). A thoughtful account of the development of the fictional detective hero after an earlier ambivalence about such figures.

Poe, Edgar Allan, 'The Philosophy of Composition', 'The Poetic Principle', Review of Hawthorne's 'Twice-Told Tales', all in *The Fall of the House of Usher and other Writings* (Harmondsworth, Middx.: Penguin, 1986). Not specifically about detective fiction, these three essays all point to the 'unity of effect' which made the Dupin stories so seminal.

Porter, Dennis, *The Pursuit of Crime: Art and Ideology in Crime Fiction* (New Haven: Yale University Press, 1981). Perhaps the best single study analysing the genre in terms of literary theory.

Priestman, Martin, *Detective Fiction and Literature: The Figure on the Carpet* (Basingstoke and London: Macmillan, 1990). Relates some of the concerns of the present study to the conventional distinction between high and low literature.

Pykett, Lyn, *The Sensation Novel: from 'The Woman in White' to 'The Moonstone'* (Plymouth: Northcote House, 1994). Intelligently discusses the 'sensation novels' of the 1860s and 1870s as a breakthrough in the fictional empowerment of women.

Reynolds, Kimberley, and Nicola Humble, *Victorian Heroines: Representations of Femininity in Nineteenth-Century Literature and Art* (New York and London: Harvester Wheatsheaf, 1993). Contains an excellent chapter on Sensation Fiction.

Slung, Michelle B (ed.), *Crime on her Mind: Fifteen Stories and Female Sleuths from the Victorian Era to the Forties* (Harmondsworth, Middx.: Penguin, 1977). An informatively introduced collection of short stories featuring female detectives, some from before the Sherlock Holmes era: a salutary reminder that the tough woman sleuth long predates 1970s feminism.

Symons, Julian, *Bloody Murder: From the Detective Story to the Crime Novel: A History* (Harmondsworth, Middx.: Penguin, 1985, 2nd edition). Majestic: the source of innumerable facts and details for this present study and I hope not too many of its ideas. While traditionalist in some emphases and conclusions, it mounts a barrage of theoretically sophisticated arguments about the genre while being as nearly comprehensive about particular examples as a study of under 250 pages could possibly be.

Todorov, Tsvetan, 'The Typology of Detective Fiction', in *The Poetics of Prose*, translated by R. Howard, (Oxford: Basil Blackwell, 1977). A deceptively simple analysis of the structure of the genre, from which the present study borrows its key categories.

Winks, Robin, W. (ed.), *Detective Fiction: A Collection of Critical Essays* (Englewood Cliffs, NJ: Prentice-Hall, 1980). Along with Haycraft and Most/Stowe (see above), should be part of everyone's essential three-pack of classic, critically alert writing on the subject. Includes key essays by W. H. Auden, Dorothy Sayers, Ross Macdonald and George Grella.

Worpole, Ken, *Dockers and Detectives* (London: Verso, 1983). Contains a useful account of the impact of hardboiled American writing on British working-class readers.

Index

Recent and
Forthcoming Titles
in the
New Series of

WRITERS AND
THEIR WORK

WRITERS AND THEIR WORK
RECENT & FORTHCOMING TITLES

Title	Author
Peter Ackroyd	*Susana Onega*
Kingsley Amis	*Richard Bradford*
W.H. Auden	*Stan Smith*
Aphra Behn	*Sue Wiseman*
Edward Bond	*Michael Mangan*
Emily Brontë	*Stevie Davies*
A.S. Byatt	*Richard Todd*
Angela Carter	*Lorna Sage*
Geoffrey Chaucer	*Steve Ellis*
Children's Literature	*Kimberley Reynolds*
Caryl Churchill	*Elaine Aston*
John Clare	*John Lucas*
S.T. Coleridge	*Stephen Bygrave*
Joseph Conrad	*Cedric Watts*
Crime Fiction	*Martin Priestman*
John Donne	*Stevie Davis*
George Eliot	*Josephine McDonagh*
English Translators of Homer	*Simeon Underwood*
Henry Fielding	*Jenny Uglow*
Elizabeth Gaskell	*Kate Flint*
William Golding	*Kevin McCarron*
Graham Greene	*Peter Mudford*
Hamlet	*Ann Thompson & Neil Taylor*
Thomas Hardy	*Peter Widdowson*
David Hare	*Jeremy Ridgman*
Tony Harrison	*Joe Kelleher*
William Hazlitt	*J. B. Priestley; R. L. Brett (intro. by Michael Foot)*
Seamus Heaney	*Andrew Murphy*
George Herbert	*T.S. Eliot (intro. by Peter Porter)*
Henry James – The Later Writing	*Barbara Hardy*
James Joyce	*Steven Connor*
Franz Kafka	*Michael Wood*
King Lear	*Terence Hawkes*
Philip Larkin	*Lawrence Lerner*
D.H. Lawrence	*Linda Ruth Williams*
Doris Lessing	*Elizabeth Maslen*
David Lodge	*Bernard Bergonzi*
Christopher Marlowe	*Thomas Healy*
Andrew Marvell	*Annabel Patterson*
Ian McEwan	*Kiernan Ryan*
A Midsummer Night's Dream	*Helen Hackett*
Walter Pater	*Laurel Brake*
Brian Patten	*Linda Cookson*
Sylvia Plath	*Elisabeth Bronfen*
Jean Rhys	*Helen Carr*
Richard II	*Margaret Healy*
Dorothy Richardson	*Carol Watts*
Romeo and Juliet	*Sasha Roberts*
Salman Rushdie	*Damien Grant*
Paul Scott	*Jacqueline Banerjee*
The Sensation Novel	*Lyn Pykett*
Edmund Spenser	*Colin Burrow*
J.R.R. Tolkien	*Charles Moseley*
Leo Tolstoy	*John Bayley*
Angus Wilson	*Peter Conradi*
Virginia Woolf	*Laura Marcus*
Working Class Fiction	*Ian Haywood*
W.B. Yeats	*Edward Larrissy*
Charlotte Yonge	*Alethea Hayter*

TITLES IN PREPARATION

Title	Author
Antony and Cleopatra	*Ken Parker*
Jane Austen	*Meenakshi Mukherjee*
Alan Ayckbourn	*Michael Holt*
J.G. Ballard	*Michel Delville*
Samuel Beckett	*Keir Elam*
William Blake	*John Beer*
Elizabeth Bowen	*Maud Ellmann*
Charlotte Brontë	*Sally Shuttleworth*
Caroline Dramatists	*Julie Sanders*
Daniel Defoe	*Jim Rigney*
Charles Dickens	*Rod Mengham*
Carol Ann Duffy	*Deryn Rees Jones*
E.M. Forster	*Nicholas Royle*
Brian Friel	*Geraldine Higgins*
The *Gawain* Poet	*John Burrow*
Gothic Literature	*Emma Clery*
Henry IV	*Peter Bogdanov*
Henrik Ibsen	*Sally Ledger*
Geoffrey Hill	*Andrew Roberts*
Kazuo Ishiguro	*Cynthia Wong*
Ben Jonson	*Anthony Johnson*
Julius Caesar	*Mary Hamer*
John Keats	*Kelvin Everest*
Rudyard Kipling	*Jan Montefiore*
Charles and Mary Lamb	*Michael Baron*
Langland: *Piers Plowman*	*Claire Marshall*
C.S. Lewis	*William Gray*
Katherine Mansfield	*Helen Haywood*
Measure for Measure	*Kate Chedgzoy*
Vladimir Nabokov	*Neil Cornwell*
Old English Verse	*Graham Holderness*
Alexander Pope	*Pat Rogers*
Dennis Potter	*Derek Paget*
Lord Rochester	*Germaine Greer*
Christina Rossetti	*Kathryn Burlinson*
Mary Shelley	*Catherine Sharrock*
P.B. Shelley	*Paul Hamilton*
Stevie Smith	*Alison Light*
Wole Soyinka	*Mpalive Msiska*
Laurence Sterne	*Manfred Pfister*
Tom Stoppard	*Nicholas Cadden*
The Tempest	*Gordon McMullan*
Charles Tomlinson	*Tim Clark*
Anthony Trollope	*Andrew Sanders*
Derek Walcott	*Stewart Brown*
John Webster	*Thomas Sorge*
Mary Wollstonecraft	*Jane Moore*
Women Romantic Poets	*Anne Janowitz*
Women Writers of the 17th Century	*Ramona Wray*
William Wordsworth	*Nicholas Roe*